Is mankind doomed to starvation and misery in the twenty-first century? Will the doubling of the world's population by the year 2000 create widespread famine? Will overpopulation bring about the ultimate catastrophe of nuclear war?

The contributors to this volume (among them Frank W. Notestein, J. George Harrar, and David E. Bell) argue that these grim consequences of hunger are not inevitable. As Clifford M. Hardin asserts, recent accomplishments hold out the hope that the world's population in the twenty-first century can be fed, and fed better than at any time in man's history. But before the threat of starvation subsides, the world's nations *must* make efforts of unprecedented magnitude to promote family planning and agricultural development.

This book explains the reform of economic, social, and political institutions essential to the total economic development of poorer nations.

As this study makes clear, drastic measures are needed *today* to prevent hunger, preserve peace, and, perhaps, to save all mankind tomorrow.

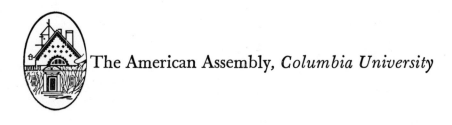

The American Assembly, *Columbia University*

OVERCOMING
WORLD HUNGER

Prentice-Hall, Inc., *Englewood Cliffs, N.J.*

Printed in the United States of America.

Current printing (last number):

10 9 8 7 6 5 4 3 2 1

PRENTICE-HALL INTERNATIONAL, INC. (*London*)

1470610
Preface

The thirty-fourth American Assembly program opened with a national meeting at Arden House, Harriman, New York, October 31–November 3, 1968. Participants in that meeting, representing a range of pursuits and viewpoints, discussed in small groups issues bearing on world hunger and malnutrition; and ·. final plenary session they approved a statement of findings an⌐   ͺations for United States policy. Printed as a sepa-
r²·   ͻrt may be obtained from The American Assembly.
  ₩ͺͺͺch follow were originally designed as background reading for participants at Arden House, under the supervision of Clifford M. Hardin, Chancellor of The University of Nebraska. They will comprise the background reading for regional Assemblies on this subject in the United States, and are also intended for the general reader.

The opinions herein are the authors' own and not necessarily those of The American Assembly, which takes no stand on matters it presents for public discussion, or of the W. K. Kellogg Foundation, whose generous grant, gratefully acknowledged herewith, made this program possible.

Clifford C. Nelson
President
The American Assembly

Table of Contents

Tables and Figures

Tables

Figures

Clifford M. Hardin, Editor

Introduction:

For Humanity, New Hope

Hope that the world's population of 2000 A.D. *can* be fed and fed *better* than in mankind's entire history arises from accomplishments recorded in the late 1960's. It is still a hope, not a certainty. But this optimistic goal is attainable with continuing, concerted efforts of unprecedented magnitude by the world's community of nations.

This is the opportunity—this is the challenge!

In this book, the authors discuss both sides of the population-food

CLIFFORD M. HARDIN *is United States Secretary of Agriculture. He served as Chancellor of The University of Nebraska for fourteen years and has taught agricultural economics at the University of Wisconsin and Michigan State University. Dr. Hardin is a member of the National Science Board and of the Executive Board of the Council on Higher Education in the American Republics. He is a former President of the National Association of State Universities and Land-Grant Colleges, and served as a member of the President's Committee to Strengthen the Security of the Free World.*

The editor wishes to acknowledge the editorial and technical assistance of Dr. Gene A. Budig, his assistant at the University of Nebraska, and Dr. Everett E. Peterson, professor of agricultural economics at the university.

equation. They make population projections and appraise present and future efforts to limit population growth. They discuss food requirements and how more food can be produced. They outline methods by which the United States and other advanced nations may most effectively assist developing nations to solve problems of growing populations.

The essential elements of a policy to solve these problems are:

1. Family, national and international policies for effective population control *now,* i.e., reducing the propensity to reproduce;
2. Agricultural development to increase food production in hungry nations, with interim food aid from advanced countries;
3. Economic, political and social changes in developing countries designed to promote total economic development.

But why should Americans be concerned with the problems of people and poverty in other countries? Quite frankly, we are concerned for both altruistic and selfish reasons. Geographic, economic and political isolation is impossible in today's world. The alternative to peaceful solutions is increasing social unrest, political instability, human misery, and possibly such worldwide catastrophes as famine and war. We are deeply concerned as:

—surplus food producers with the ability and capacity to expand output quickly and greatly;
—businessmen who supply farm production items, provide marketing facilities, or desire expanding foreign markets for industrial products;
—consumers whose level of living is raised by unrestricted international movement of goods and services;
—taxpayers who pay the costs of public programs for food aid, technical assistance and military preparedness in a troubled world;
—people being asked by our churches and other organizations for greater voluntary contributions to support overseas programs;
—citizens of a democracy with responsibilities for determining public policies;
—humanitarians interested in human dignity and rights and seeking to alleviate injustice, hunger and misery anywhere in the world.

People interested in world affairs are now well aware of the rapid growth rate in population, especially in the developing countries.

They realize that, as a result of dramatic declines in death rates without corresponding decreases in birth rates, the world's population in the year 2000 may be double that of 1965, or six to seven billion people. Population projections, geographical distribution of people and birth control are discussed in Chapter 1 of this book.

It will take twice as much food by 2000 A.D. to feed twice as many people no better than the people of the 1960's were fed. To provide nutritionally adequate diets for six to seven billion people will require much more food, especially more protein. The second chapter in this book gives estimates of future food needs of the world's people, not only to feed them but also to feed them better. Chapter 3 describes some recent developments in agricultural technology—the payoff from years of pioneering and continuing work of the Rockefeller and W. K. Kellogg foundations, and the impact of the programs of The Ford Foundation, the U.S. Department of Agriculture, the U.S. Agency for International Development, the American land-grant universities, the Food and Agriculture Organization of the United Nations, and technical assistance programs of individual nations. It also points out the physical and economic requirements for full realization of the potential benefits of this technology. Chapter 4 suggests new and expanded public policies and programs needed for limiting population growth, increasing food production and improving human nutrition.

Research is under way, and will continue, on the physical and economic feasibility of obtaining more protein from marine life and other nonagricultural sources. While a major breakthrough is possible, it is probable that, for the remainder of this century at least, most of the increased food consumed by the world's people will come from farm land and most of the food needed in countries with rapidly growing populations will come from the agricultural resources of those same nations.

The near famine in India of 1965–66, averted only by massive shipments of grain from the United States, aroused widespread concern over whether the world could feed its people at existing levels of nutrition in hungry nations even with all-out food production in advanced countries. Favorable weather, the wider adoption of

higher yielding food-grain varieties and associated production
practices, and greater emphasis upon agricultural development by
food-deficit nations apparently have provided *some* lead time in
which to solve the food and other problems associated with more
and more people.

Projections of grain production and consumption made recently
by the U.S. Department of Agriculture imply that the world
viewed as a whole could continue to have excess grain producing
capacity to 1980, and that problems of food shortage would be
caused by differences in productive capacity among nations and by
food distribution problems among and within countries. The study
concludes that chronic excess grain production is not likely to
materialize because: trade barriers would be reduced; production
would be limited in exporting nations; and concessional exports to
certain developing countries will continue.[1]

This temporary reprieve from food crises does not permit a return to complacency and indifference without risking the strong
possibility of serious food shortages by 1985, or 2000, or 2025. Food
aid has "bought time" but is not a permanent solution to the world's
food problem either for the donor or the recipient nations; it may
actually retard agricultural development in the latter countries.
American farmers demonstrated in 1967 that they can—and will—
expand production in response to price, patriotism and people's
needs, but they expect to be paid for their efforts just as other producers expect returns on resources used. The *need* for food without
purchasing power does not generate effective economic demand for
food from surplus producing nations unless paid for by the taxpayers
of advanced countries.

While the emphasis in this publication is upon population, food
and economic growth for the developing nations, it is recognized
that other serious problems arise as populations grow, both in the
advanced and developing countries. In some areas people are now
competing for space as well as sustenance.

[1] Abel, Martin E., and Rojko, Anthony S., *World Food Situation,* Foreign
Agricultural Economic Report No. 35, U.S.D.A., Washington, D.C., 1967.

Increasing urbanization characterizes the geographical distribution of the growing populations in both advanced and developing nations. As people crowd into cities, the problems of housing, water supplies, sewage disposal, electricity, streets, police and fire protection intensify, in addition to those of food, employment, education, medical services and recreational facilities. Rural-urban migrants often are poorly prepared for the emotional stresses of urban living, the decline in family importance and other social, economic and political changes.

Recent studies and events on the American scene dramatize the stubborn persistence of "pockets" of poverty, disease, malnutrition and ignorance even in the world's most affluent society. Because the problems of poverty and malnutrition in large cities and depressed rural areas are not treated specifically in this publication does not mean that they are deemed to be unimportant. Rather it is recognized that they require separate and special consideration. Here in the United States there is enough food and enough of the right kinds. The problem is how to get it to the people who need it.

All of these problems must be worked on simultaneously if the world community is to move toward the goals of peace, progress and prosperity in the years ahead.

The President's Panel on the World Food Supply reached four basic conclusions in regard to the deteriorating condition of two-thirds of the world's people. They are:

1. The scale, severity and duration of the world food problem are so great that a massive, long-range, innovative effort unprecedented in human history will be required to master it.

2. The solution of the problem that will exist after about 1985 demands that programs of population control be initiated now. For the immediate future, the food supply is critical.

3. Food supply is directly related to agricultural deveopment and, in turn, agricultural development and overall economic development are critically interdependent in the hungry countries.

4. A strategy for attacking the world food problem will, of necessity, encompass the entire foreign economic assistance effort of the United

States in concert with other developed countries, voluntary institutions, and international organizations.[2]

Thus, the objectives are recognized, the methods are becoming known and some time is available for solving the population explosion problems of the twentieth century. What is needed is an effective strategy for implementing programs in line with policy goals. To develop a strategy for dealing seriously and productively with the problems of international development, the Panel recommended:

1. The American public must be convinced that the efforts merit investment of their taxes and that the efforts will be effective in meeting the overall problem.
2. The American public must have confidence in the substance of the programs which are implemented and in the arm of the government which is responsible for administration of those programs.
3. Funding and programs must be placed on a long-range basis, not budgeted and funded hand-to-mouth, from year to year. Foreign economic assistance is doomed to frustration and failure if the responsible agency is forced to deal only with quick payoff projects and to show results tomorrow in order to survive the next budget cycle.[3]

Similar recommendations are made by the National Council of Churches, the Church World Service, the National Advisory Commission on Food and Fiber, and in many other statements on the world's population, food requirements and poverty. As an administrative officer of a land-grant university, I am keenly aware of the urgent need for a long-range commitment by our government to a program for training an international service corps of agricultural research and extension specialists if our—the universities'—efforts in foreign agricultural development are to be more effective. The problems of more people are long run in nature, taking at least the remainder of this century to solve, and requiring large-scale continuing programs rather than "crash" programs.

[2] *The World Food Problem,* A report of the President's Science Advisory Committee, Vol. I, The White House, May, 1967, p. 11.
[3] *Ibid.,* p. 24.

The tasks that still confront us in problem areas of world food, technical assistance and economic development are proving to be more difficult, more complex, and more long lasting than we imagined when the Marshall Plan was initiated in 1948. The temptation is strong to turn inward, to concentrate on domestic problems while relying upon our geographical location and military strength to protect us from social and political upheavals elsewhere in the world. The purposes of this book are: to increase understanding of the nature and magnitude of the world's population-food problems; to review the possibilities and obstacles to decelerating population growth and accelerating food production; and to outline the policy and resource requirements to eliminate hunger from the earth.

Frank W. Notestein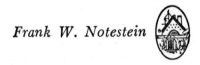

1

Population Growth
and Its Control

Making Population Projections

PROBLEMS AND USES

From one point of view it is virtually impossible to predict the future population of the world or of its several parts. From another, it is quite simple. The difference turns on the amount of precision required for the problem at hand. It is impossible to forecast the future population of any particular part of the world with much accuracy. If a prediction is accurate, the result reflects luck

FRANK W. NOTESTEIN *is President Emeritus of The Population Council. Formerly Professor of Demography and Director of the Office of Population Research, Princeton University, he served also as the first Director of the Population Division of the Bureau of Social Affairs of the United Nations. Dr. Notestein has also been advisor to the Minister of Health of India. He is a past President of the Population Association of America, a member of the American Statistical Association, of the American Association for the Advancement of Science, of the International Union for the Scientific Study of Population, and of the International Statistical Institute.*

quite as much as either science or wisdom. The difficulty is, of course, that future social, economic and political events will affect the future components of population change, i.e., fertility, mortality and migration.

Often other scholars ask the demographer to forecast the future demographic position so that they can examine the social, economic and political consequences of that position. Of course, it is equally true that the demographer would like social, economic and political forecasts in order to examine their demographic consequences. The fact is that none of the elements of the problem are independent of the others. Economic, social, political and demographic trends form, in their biological setting, a network of interrelated causes and consequences. In a real sense nothing can be foreseen with precision until all is foreseen.

Fortunately, from a more practical point of view these barriers to the attainment of precision in forecasting are often not very important. When we are planning for the distant future, the only planning that has practical significance is in very broad outline. Mainly we need to know the directions of change, and something of its expected general magnitude. Indeed, we could make rather little use of precise forecasts if we had them because in a complicated world the margins of uncertainty must remain large. Planning for the distant future cannot be closely calibrated.

Frequently, also, the nature of the question posed introduces simplifying conditions. Generally we are not asked what the future population will be; instead, we are asked for a model showing what the population would be under certain conditions. It is this kind of projection that is needed as background for considerations of future problems of hunger and nutrition. For example, it is all too probable that between now and the end of the century there will be a full-scale war between major powers in which modern engines of destruction will kill a substantial proportion of the human race. The risk is real, because the knowledge of the means is too widely distributed to allow an easy assumption that nothing will go wrong. There is certainly an appreciable chance that major sections of the population will, in effect, be killed by nuclear accident. One could be concerned with the demography of this catastrophe as a background for plans to cope with recovery.

But for our present problem all such considerations are irrelevant. Since we are considering problems of hunger and nutrition from the point of view of long-range planning for the elimination of hunger and the improvement of nutrition, it makes no sense to consider such problems in a context in which planning is impossible. Present production plans will surely be irrelevant in the absence of peace. Our problem then is not what will be, but what will be *if* there is a generally peaceful and orderly world for which planning is possible.

There are other constraints on our projection of the demographic future that are implicit in the problem. We need not, indeed we must not, estimate future trends in mortality on the assumption of major losses from starvation or malnutrition. Such losses are occurring, and may well be substantial in several parts of the world during the balance of this century. But these possibilities are irrelevant if our planning is for the world. In estimating the future need for food, we cannot use projections that incorporate implicitly a grossly inadequate food supply. Planners must be prepared to face the consequences of their own success. In this sense our projections should go further than implying no loss of life through starvation and gross malnutrition. Population projections to be used as one element in calculating future needs for food should be based on a rather optimistic judgment of future possibilities in the reduction of death rates.

In sum, our task is not that of saying what population will be, but what it will be *if* there is a generally orderly and peaceful future in which rising nutritional status helps with the progressive curtailment of disease. Since, within these assumptions, we seek the dimensions of the food problem, the essential questions are:

1. How many people will the future bring, and at what rates of change, in the major sections of the world and in the major age groups of the population?
2. To what extent could these numbers and rates be reduced by conscious efforts to spread the control of fertility?

Or, more generally, what is the expected demographic load, and what can be done to reduce it in the context of improving health?

Even with these simplified conditions a high degree of accuracy is not to be expected. One is, in effect, trying to foresee what the trends of fertility, mortality and migration will be under the specified conditions. These trends, in turn, will depend on the stage of economic and social development, and on the rates of social-economic change as well as on the nature of any explicit population policy. At best we may hope to foresee something of the general nature and something of the tempo of population change. Indeed, our knowledge is so inadequate that no two people of equal background would independently give the same detailed forecast; on the other hand, most knowledgeable demographers would tend to treat the prospects of the world's several regions in the same way. Given such uncertainty there seems little use in putting forward a new set of population projections. Instead, I propose to base the discussion on the projections in *World Population Prospects, As Assessed in 1963*. United Nations Population Studies, No. 41 (New York: United Nations, 1966).

The work is generally satisfactory and will serve as a point of departure. On health, its implicit assumptions are reasonably optimistic. Its regional estimates assume that the expectation of life at birth rises from the present position by one-half a year per year with diminishing rates of gain at high levels, and no gain beyond 73.9 for the sexes combined. Since these are forecasts for regions, the implicit assumption is that the more advanced countries within the region achieve even higher levels.

It is to be noted that there is also the implicit assumption that no further major medical innovations are going to be of practical importance before the end of the century. Such innovations would have little effect at ages below 50, since the virtual elimination of death below age 50 turns more on the need for action than on the need for knowledge. Innovations that will make major differences probably will arise only in the older ages, and they are likely to come rather slowly and to be very expensive. If they have substantial effect by the end of the century it will almost certainly be in the highly modernized parts of the world for which nutritional problems should not prove difficult to solve. The mortality assumptions may be conservative, but if so they are conservative in ways that are not very important for problems of food and nutrition.

The assumptions about the course of fertility are more complicated. The treatment is completely different for the Less-Developed than for the More-Developed Regions. In the former, the gross reproduction rates are well above 2; that is, a perpetuation of the age-specific rates of bearing female children would, in the absence of death, give twice as many daughters as there were women in the maternal generation. For them the assumption is that fertility will fall, once the decline starts, to about one-half of the initial level, generally in about thirty years. But the starting times are highly variable. In the case of areas with little urbanization and strong tribal organization, notably in parts of Africa, the length of time assumed to be required for a 50 per cent reduction in fertility is substantially lengthened and the beginning of the decline comes late. In fact the Medium assumption implies virtually no reduction in fertility in Africa except in the Northern and Southern regions. In general the High and Low assumptions utilize the same pattern of decline, but with later and earlier dates of onset than that hypothesized in the Medium projections.

For the More-Developed Regions the assumptions about fertility are simpler. These are the countries in which the gross reproduction rate is well below 2. The High variant carried the assumption that after 1970 the birth rates would be 25 per 1,000 population in the countries where fertility is now moderately low, and 20 per 1,000 in countries where fertility is now very low. The Low assumption from 1970 on for these two groups is 18 and 16 respectively, and the Medium course is in between. A good many of the countries in both categories are now below even the Low level assumed for 1970 and subsequent years.

For the regional projections, migration is taken to be important only in the case of Europe as an area of origin and the Americas and Oceania as regions of destination.

Not much can be said in favor of the realism of such arbitrary manipulations of the future rates of birth, death and migration, except that nothing better is possible. Nevertheless, these assumed changes in the vital rates are not the factors that mainly determine the outcome by 2000. The outcome is principally determined by the initial population, the age structure, the base rates of fertility, mortality and migration, and the direction of the changes assumed for them. The magnitudes of change also count, of course, but unless they are somewhat drastic they are less important. The outcome by the end of the century is principally determined by the initial population, the initial structure of vital rates and the direction of changes.

The major difficulty with the U.N. projections arises with Mainland East Asia, which is dominated by China. China has never had a census that can stand critical scrutiny. It is not outside the bounds of possibility that the real figure for 1960 differs by as much as 100 million from that used by the U.N., and one would like to know the direction of the deviation. There is equally no direct evidence about the death rate or the birth rate. The values used come from inadequate scattered surveys made generally by methods almost guaranteed to give an understatement of both birth and death. The initial values selected for both mortality and fertility seem strange to me. It is quite likely that the birth rate of Mainland East Asia is as high as that of South Asia, but the initial rate implied by the U.N. is 32.6 per 1,000 population for Mainland East Asia and 43.0 for South Asia. Even in Taiwan, where the population is prosperous, urban and literate, and there is a strong birth control effort, the rate did not go below 32.0 until 1966. For mortality, the initial rate is the same as that for South Asia, but the rate of improvement is less rapid. The result is that between 1960 and 2000 the Medium variants project an average annual rate of population growth of 1.2 per cent for Mainland East Asia, and 2.3 per cent for South Asia.

Such differences are important. For example, if Mainland East

Asia were to be given the growth of the Medium variant for South
Asia, its population would be about 600 million larger than that
shown in its Medium projection. It seems to me reasonable to conclude that, on the assumptions of public order and reasonably
adequate food, the projection for Mainland East Asia, and cor-
respondingly that for the Less-Developed Regions and The World,
may well be 600 million too small by the year 2000.

Although the basic data leave much to be desired in the remainder
of the Less-Developed Regions there are no difficulties of the
magnitude presented by China. There may be substantial errors,
but at present the guesses seem rather reasonable.

Once the initial population is available, classified by age and sex,
and the assumptions regarding mortality, fertility and migration
have been decided upon, the projection is obtained in five-year steps
by subtracting estimated deaths from each age group and adding
the survivors from estimated births to the population under age
five. Since for the most part it is assumed that fertility will decline,
the population tends to increase a little more rapidly in the earlier
than in the later years. However, the main factor is the height of
the rates and not their changes. The average annual rate of change
for the years 1960 to 2000 can, therefore, be used to give the intervening projections with seldom more than 2 per cent and never more
than 4 per cent discrepancy.

Projections and Their Implications

What, then, do the projections show for the world? They
are summarized for the major regions in Table 1. The suggested
average annual rates of growth for the world's population between
1960 and 2000 range from 1.5 per cent for the Low value, through
the Medium value of 1.8 per cent, to the High value of 2.1 per
cent. If Mainland East Asia grows like South Asia the values become 1.8, 2.0, and 2.3 per cent respectively. From 3 billion in 1960
the numbers rise by the end of the century to a Low of 5.5 billion,
a Medium value of about 6 billion and a High value of 7 billion.
More sensible values for Mainland East Asia would add between

TABLE 1. *Estimated Population, 1920 & 1960, and Projected 1980 & 2000 by Regions, in Millions**

	Estimated		Projected	2000			Average Annual Growth Rate: Medium Projection
	1920	1960	1980 Med.	Med.	Low	High	1960–2000**
The World	1,860	2,998	4,330	6,130	5,449	6,994	1.8
Less-Developed Regions	1,187	2,022	3,136	4,688	4,155	5,420	2.1
East Asia (ex. Japan)	498	701	930	1,165	1,003	1,484	1.3
If Mainland East Asia grows at rate projected for South Asia:							
The World			4,554	6,726	6,056	7,496	2.0
Less-Developed Regions			3,360	5,284	4,762	5,922	2.4
East Asia (ex. Japan)			1,154	1,761	1,610	1,986	2.3
South Asia	470	865	1,420	2,171	1,984	2,444	2.3
Melanesia, Micronesia & Polynesia	2	3	5	7	6	9	2.3
Africa	143	273	449	768	684	864	2.6
Latin America (ex. Temperate South America)	75	179	332	577	477	619	2.9
More Developed Regions	673	976	1,194	1,441	1,293	1,574	1.0
Europe	325	425	479	527	491	563	.5
U.S.S.R.	155	214	278	353	316	403	1.3
Northern America	116	199	262	354	294	376	1.4
Japan	55	93	111	122	115	139	.7

TABLE I. *Continued*

	Estimated		Projected				Average Annual Growth Rate: Medium Projection 1960–2000**
	1920	1960	1980 Med.	2000 Med.	Low	High	
Temperate South America	15	33	46	61	55	67	1.5
Australia & New Zealand	7	13	18	24	22	26	1.6

** Computed by the author from data given in thousands. If these average rates are applied for five year intervals according to the formula $P_t = P_o e^{rt}$, the resulting projected populations for the years intervening between 1960 and 2000 tend to be lower than the U.N. projected values, but the difference is seldom more than 2 per cent and never more than 4 per cent. The maximum departures occur about 1980. The formula is that for compound interest when the compounding is continuous instead of annual, P_t is the population t years after P_o, the initial population, r is the annual rate, and e is the base of the natural logarithms.

* Source: The United Nations, *World Population Prospects as Assessed in 1963*, Population Studies, No. 41, New York, 1966. Sales No.: 66.XIII.2.

500 and 600 million to these figures. In short, by the year 2000, the world has an excellent chance of requiring food for more than twice the present population.

It is also clear from Table 1 that the projected growth is more than twice as high for the Less-Developed Regions as for the More-Developed Regions. In the latter the average rate is 1.0 per cent, and that figure may well be too high. In the former it is 2.1 per cent. Moreover, if we lift the rather doubtful figure for Mainland East Asia, the average rate for the Less-Developed Regions becomes 2.4 per cent, a rate that if maintained doubles the population in less than 29 years. The projections suggest a slightly slower rate of growth in South Asia than in Tropical Latin America and Africa. The faster growth projected for Tropical Latin America than for

Africa arises from reduced death rates and in spite of the faster decline of fertility than that projected for Africa.

The More-Developed Regions are projected to grow at an average rate of 1.0 per cent. It is possible that the rate will actually go lower; indeed it is now below the projected level in both Northern America and the U.S.S.R. The actual course of events seems likely to lie between 0.5 per cent and 1.0 per cent. Since these are the parts of the world where disease is best controlled, the rate of growth will depend on the birth rate. Moreover, since this is the region in which there is widespread birth control and abortion, much will depend on the psychological climate and governmental policies. It is clear, however, that the More-Developed Regions do not face the end of growth in this century, but that they have a sufficient basis of prosperity to be able to cope with any rate of growth that is likely to emerge. Perhaps for these regions a 40 per cent increase by the end of the century is the maximum to be expected. It is also to be noted that the population of the Less-Developed Regions, which constituted 67 per cent of the world's total in 1960, is projected on the Medium variant to constitute 79 per cent of the world's total by the end of the century.

The Less-Developed Regions not only are experiencing rapid growth, they also carry a very heavy load of youth dependency, as may be seen in Table 2. In 1960, 40 per cent of the total population of the Less-Developed Regions was under 15 years of age, and if we drop the doubtful figures for Mainland East Asia the figure rises to almost 42 per cent. By contrast, in the More-Developed Regions less than 29 per cent were under 15 years of age. Since the Medium course projects a reduction in fertility, the projected proportions for 2000 are considerably lower. Table 2 also shows that the proportion of persons in the working years of life is much lower in the Less-Developed than in the More-Developed Regions, and that on the projected Medium course it may be expected to rise considerably. There are also sharp increases, particularly in the More-Developed Regions, of the population over 65 years of age. It is here that unforeseen developments in the field of medical technology may well

TABLE 2. *Percentage Distribution of Population By Broad Age Groups as Estimated for 1960 and Projected to 2000 (U.N. Medium Values)*

	Under 15		15–64		65+	
	1960	2000	1960	2000	1960	2000
The World	36.4	32.4	58.7	61.2	4.9	6.4
Less-Developed Regions	40.1	34.6	56.6	60.6	3.3	4.8
East Asia (ex. Japan)	36.9	27.3	59.1	66.0	4.0	6.7
Alternative*						
The World*	37.4	33.8	57.9	60.3	4.7	5.9
Less-Developed Regions*	41.6	36.1	55.4	59.6	3.0	4.3
East Asia (ex. Japan)*	41.2	34.4	55.8	61.0	3.0	4.6
South Asia	41.0	34.6	55.9	60.9	3.1	4.6
Melanesia, Micronesia & Polynesia	38.1	41.6	58.4	54.6	3.7	3.8
Africa	43.1	42.3	54.2	54.5	2.7	3.2
Latin America (ex. Temperate South America)	43.4	39.1	53.6	57.1	3.0	3.8
More-Developed Regions	28.7	25.6	63.0	63.0	8.3	11.4
Europe	25.7	22.9	64.5	64.0	9.8	13.1
U.S.S.R.	30.8	27.1	63.0	61.7	6.2	11.2
Northern America	31.3	29.8	59.7	61.3	9.0	8.9
Japan	29.9	19.0	64.4	67.3	5.7	13.7
Temperate So. America	32.5	29.9	62.6	63.2	4.9	8.9
Australia & New Zealand	30.6	29.6	60.9	61.0	8.5	9.4

* The values were obtained on the assumption that Mainland East Asia had the same projected rates of growth and initial age distribution as South Asia, a situation that seems more probable than the values given for Mainland East Asia in the U.N. report from which the data are taken: *World Population Prospects As Assessed in 1963*, Population Studies, No. 41, New York, 1966.

yield a sharper increase than that projected. However, throughout the world these expected trends will increase the proportions of the population in the working ages and do so especially in the Less-Developed Regions.

A CRITIQUE OF RESULTS

Now in all this there is the risk that we are playing verbal games rather than spelling out the nature of the real future. We are using figures that are much more definite than can be supported by the generalizations on which they are based. The Medium projection assumes a considerable reduction of fertility everywhere except in Africa and in the More-Developed Regions. In the latter the rationale is that the decline has taken place already. In the Less-Developed Regions the theory is that when countries with traditionally uncontrolled fertility undergo a rapid process of modernization and public education, fertility will fall by about one-half in a generation. This was roughly the case of the U.S.S.R. and Japan. In short, the decline suggested by the U.N. is the staff's best guess as to the course of events on the assumption that there is modernization but no particular governmental effort to reduce or to lift birth rates. The Medium variant is their best guess as to what may happen by a transition to low fertility which comes as a kind of automatic by-product of the modernizing process.

On these assumptions, for the reasons already suggested, I would prefer a higher figure for Mainland East Asia, where it seems to me that the initial birth rate is much too low, and where the projected decline of the death rate is too slow. Personally, I prefer an average annual rate of 2.4 per cent for the Less-Developed Regions. That gives 5.3 billion by the year 2000, and an increase of 3.3 billion, or 160 per cent, in the 40 years from 1960 to 2000.

For the More-Developed Regions, on the contrary, it seems to me that the Medium projection is a bit too high. Birth rates are now below the levels projected for the U.S.S.R. and the United States. Perhaps a Medium average annual rate of growth of 0.8 per cent would be better than the projected 1.0 per cent. The supporting evidence, however, is so extremely tenuous that it does not seem worthwhile to put forward another figure. If we modify the figure for the Less-Developed Regions, and retain that for the More-Developed Regions, the total comes to 6.7 billion by the end of the century, which is about 600 million above the U.N. Medium value, and 300 million below the U.N. High projection. On this reckoning the world, which added 1.1 billion in the 40 years after 1920, will add 3.7 billion in the 40 years after 1960.

We should stop a moment to reconsider. The above figures seem incredibly high. However, it should be recalled that the reductions in mortality projected for the future are entirely realistic in the light of past experience if we are to have an orderly future without major starvation. Moreover, the projections assume that the gross reproduction rate will be cut in half over a thirty-year period beginning at variable dates. The population increase comes in spite of the fact that the birth rate is projected to decline between 1965–1970 and 1995–2000, from 40 to 30 per 1,000 in Latin America and from 43 to 32 in South Asia. In Africa the change is only from 46 to 40, but clearly also one would expect a slower decline there. In short, no one knows what will happen, but we do know that even if birth rates decline substantially in the Less-Developed Regions those regions face a staggering increase of population in the next 40 years. It is my personal impression that the birth rates will drop, and that we can, therefore, think of the adjusted Medium projection as a reasonably high figure. If that is true, prudent planning calls for generating by the end of this century the food supply for a world population of 6.7 billion, of whom some 79 per cent will be found in today's Less-Developed Regions.

SMALL RETRENCHMENT MARGINS

There is another demographic fact that is highly pertinent. In much of today's Less-Developed Regions, and especially in Asia and Africa, the margins of health protection are pathetically thin. Millions are living close to the minimum for survival, with small room for retrenchment when trouble comes. A fairly small swing in supplies moves the situation from normal to catastrophic. We have seen India, for example, swing from the brink of starvation to a market glut of grain in one year. Neither are the barriers to the renewed spread of epidemic disease securely held in troubled times. It would not take a great deal of civil strife, political disorganization and disrupted transportation to break down the barriers to both disease and starvation. Something of this kind may have happened in China. During the war and its aftermath it did happen in part of West Java, where rather little disorganization apparently resulted in the death of about half of the population from starvation and disease.

It is my own belief that the greatest risk of loss of life facing the Less-Developed Regions is not that of malnutrition, or of slow starvation from a food supply that just barely falls short of the traditional requirements. The greatest threat is that the loss of political coherence will bring a breakdown of public order, tripping off both famine and epidemic as in Biafra for example.

This risk is real. What has almost universally been identified as an era of rising expectations in the Less-Developed Regions is becoming the era of mounting frustration. People who want, and have been promised, better living conditions, see their hopes dashed year after year. Without measurable improvements in diet and in other living conditions, there is a risk of widespread disorder, political disintegration, and starvation and disease. It seems to me there is a paradoxical risk that a food supply which just keeps up with population growth will be inadequate to prevent mass starvation. I think that in the next 40 years the choice does not lie between starvation and a subsistence diet; rather, it lies between rapidly improving diets and a mass loss of life. Prudence dictates that we plan not just a food supply, but a good food supply for about 6.7 billion people by the end of the century.

POPULATION GROWTH AND ECONOMIC DEVELOPMENT

The retention of political coherence, of course, requires more than an improving food supply. Popular frustrations relate to all elements of their living conditions—housing, clothing, medical care, education, employment and food supply. In this sense, gains in all aspects of the economy and society are essential if the risks of disorder and starvation are to be minimized. Here again the demographic factors come into play. Country after country has seen its best economic efforts almost nullified by the added burdens of rapid population growth. Schools are built and teachers trained, but the child population increases so rapidly that there are more illiterates than ever before. Houses are built, but the slums expand. Jobs are created, but the unemployed and the underemployed grow in numbers.

This is not the place for a systematic discussion of the economics of population growth, but the governing factors seem crystal clear in the Less-Developed Regions. Country after country is making a valiant effort to modernize, and considerable successes have been achieved in terms of total national income. A few countries have had sustained annual increases of more than 5 per cent in economic production. Many more have gained by less than 5 per cent. With a stationary population, a 5 per cent annual gain in national income would double per capita income in about 12 years. Since incomes per head are often under $200, and sometimes under $100 a year, even a doubling will leave the population in abject poverty. In fact, however, the populations are not stationary. As we have seen in the Less-Developed Regions the projected average growth is 2.4 per cent per year. If total income is rising by 5 per cent, and the population is growing by 2.4 per cent, then per capita income is rising by only 2.6 per cent. The pathetically low average incomes will take 27 years to double, while a doubled population takes only 29 years. A more typical situation, however, is that in which total income is rising by 4 per cent, which, with 2.4 per cent population growth, lifts per capita income by only 1.6 per cent. That requires 43 years to double. In the time it takes per capita income to rise from, say, the $200 to the $400 level, the population increases almost threefold.

The foregoing illustrations are valid unless the population growth itself helps stimulate economic growth. Here we face the fact that in most of the Less-Developed Regions there is much underemployment and much unemployment. Land, in the sense of land ready to cultivate, is mostly in short supply, as is capital which must serve as its substitute. The fact is that slower rates of population growth would in most cases make it easier to accumulate capital in the form of productive equipment, education and health protection. Slower growth is likely, therefore, to stimulate the growth of total economic product, and larger total production for more slowly growing populations means more rapidly increasing per capita incomes.

There is an urgent need to reduce the rate of population growth as an aid to the modernizing process in industry as well as in agriculture; and, indeed, it is on the success of the modernizing process in both the agricultural and the nonagricultural sectors that the hope for civil order and political coherence depends. From this point of view, reductions in the rate of population growth are as important in fostering economic development generally as they are in reducing the strain on the national food supply.

One does not have to look further to see why political leaders, knowing that the aspirations of their peoples cannot be satisfied by imperceptible improvements in living conditions, are beginning to attend anxiously to the problems of population growth. There is a widespread interest in the control of human fertility, particularly in Asia. Success in this matter might permit us to hope for lower values than those given in the Medium projections. Before trying to suggest an alternative course of growth, however, it will be well to look at the elements that seem to be moving the situation in that direction, and to some of the obstacles.

The Reduction of Fertility—Aids and Obstacles

POPULATION POLICIES

It is often asserted that family planning is a rationalistic conception completely foreign to the cultures and governments of the Less-Developed Regions—something that the modern West is trying to foist off on its poor relations to avoid the need for helping with economic development. This line has been characteristic of the more conventional Communist and Catholic writers. Nothing can be further from the truth. Rather few of the countries of the modern West have national policies designed to foster the practice of birth control. They mainly made their transitions from high to low birth rates gradually, in an era when death rates were declining so slowly that they seldom faced rates of population growth higher than 1.0 per cent per year during their early stages of modernization. (The United States is a conspicuous exception, but it had an empty and accessible continent to develop, a good deal of foreign capital, and a flexible institutional base. Even under these circumstances it is not at all clear that per capita income was increasing during the period of most rapid growth.) The European countries never had to face an urgent need to cut rates of growth that seldom reached as much as 1.0 per cent per year. As we have seen, in today's Less-Developed Regions the control of disease has become so efficient that when coupled with the high fertility of the traditional peasant societies it yields rates of growth seldom found in the world's history. In the face of such growth most of the governments of Asia have become interested in birth control. Today, something like 72 per cent of the population of the Less-Developed Regions live under governments that formally favor the reduction of birth rates as a matter of national policy. At least that is the case if we count Mainland China, which does not talk about the birth rate but does talk about responsible parenthood, urges delayed marriage, permits sterilization and abortion under rather liberal circumstances, and appears to be trying to make contraceptive information and supplies available to the public.

Countries with firmly expressed policies include: Pakistan, Nepal, India, Ceylon, Nationalist China (Taiwan), South Korea, Iran, Malaysia, Turkey, Egypt, Tunisia, Morocco, Kenya, Costa Rica, Trinidad and Tobago, El Salvador, Jamaica and Barbados. Substantial efforts to promote birth control are being made with the active co-operation of governmental and quasi-governmental institutions in Thailand, Indonesia, the Philippines, Colombia, Venezuela, Chile and Peru. These lists doubtless will have grown before they appear in print. The important fact, however, is that governmental efforts to spread the practice of family planning are much stronger in the Less-Developed than in the More-Developed Regions. The situation is the more remarkable in that ten years ago India was the only government of the Less-Developed Regions that had such a formal policy.

Of course, the existence of national policies on paper does not guarantee national programs that have substance. On the contrary, in the field of family planning, as in that of economic and agricultural development, a good game is talked long before it is played.

The policies tend to be introduced in response to particular pressures, such as those from the planning boards. They tend to be passively accepted, but initially without much deep conviction in other parts of the government, especially when the programs begin to compete for scarce personnel and funds. The initial efforts are likely, therefore, to be ill-financed, ill-manned and ineffective. In this Taiwan and South Korea are conspicuous exceptions, but in general it seems to take something like five years of halfhearted attempts before the program gains enough support to be taken seriously. One should not be surprised that such innovative efforts take time to organize and mount; indeed, the reverse would be surprising.

In many parts of the world, but notably in Latin America, the problem of illegal abortion has also been a powerful stimulus for family planning programs. Throughout much of Latin America there remains the view that the continent is empty, and needs much more population if its resources are to be adequately used. That it can support much larger populations if it modernizes, all would agree. (Of course, at its present rates of growth, in 84 years it would have a larger population than the Less-Developed Regions now have altogether.) Most students feel that a reduction of the rate of population growth would speed the process of modernization. But this is not the traditional view, which throughout the ages has tended to view "bigger" as synonymous with "better." The economic arguments for lower fertility are less effective than in Asia. But the fact that in nation after nation the hospitals are filled and the medical services overloaded with cases of septic abortion, makes a large impression on the essentially Catholic leadership. Interest in family planning is mounting rapidly, but the interests of governments tend to lag behind those of the people.

While both economic and medical considerations are doing much to strengthen interest in family planning programs, other factors are moving in the same direction.

NEW METHODS OF CONTRACEPTION

Ten years ago most of the leaders of the Less-Developed Regions felt convinced that the available contraceptive methods would never be accepted by their peoples. One of the reasons for the lack of energy in the early efforts of India and Pakistan was this belief that the available methods were simply not appropriate.

This situation has changed dramatically in the past five years. To-day there are two classes of methods that are safe, relatively inexpensive, highly effective, and have the great advantage of requiring no attention at the time of coitus. They have given contraceptive technology entirely new dimensions. Before long they will almost certainly be supplemented, if not replaced, by still more appropriate methods. These developments have convinced many leaders that it will indeed be worth while to mount serious birth control programs.

Thus far, national family planning programs in the Less-Developed Regions have relied mainly on the new form of plastic intrauterine devices, principally the Lippes Loop. In absolute terms it is less effective than the oral steroids (the Pill), which when taken methodically are 100 per cent effective. The intrauterine device (IUD), however, has the advantage that once in place no further attention is required for those who tolerate it. In actual use, because there is no problem of patient neglect, the IUD has much the same degree of effectiveness as the Pill.

The difficulty with the IUD is that perhaps 20–30 per cent of women cannot tolerate it because of discomfort or bleeding. The levels of discontinuation depend in part on the skill and training of physicians, as is shown by the fact that continuation rates vary sharply from physician to physician. Indeed, it is clear that present difficulties can be considerably reduced as the training of medical and paramedical personnel improves. Nevertheless, careful studies conducted under the sponsorship of The Population Council suggest that after two years something like 50 per cent of the patients are wearing the original device. Reinsertions after initial ejections add another 5–10 per cent, so that at present something between 55 and 60 per cent of the acceptors are protected for two years. Obviously this is far from a perfect record. But, obviously also, to have 55–60 per cent of the acceptors practicing extremely effective contraception after two years is a considerable achievement. Moreover, those who discontinue have all the conventional alternatives available. Indeed, in Taiwan there is clear evidence that those who discontinued did not, for the most part, revert to the unprotected state. Some were sterilized, others had abortions, and still others changed to other contraceptives. The acceptors who began with the IUD showed a sharply reduced childbearing performance.

The IUD is far from the perfect contraceptive, but in the Less-Developed Regions it has done much to lift birth control from an area of hope to that of a practical program. Now, some seven years after The Population Council made its first grants in support of research on the IUD, at least seven million women have been fitted with them, and they are now being manufactured in South Korea, Taiwan, Hong Kong, India, Egypt, Pakistan and Turkey, and in all of them at a cost of less than three cents each.

The oral steroids have been very important in the United States, Canada, Australia, New Zealand and Britain. They are now spreading in Europe and among the upper classes in Latin America. They have not thus far been very important in the Less-Developed Regions, mainly because they have until recently been too expensive. This situation is now drastically changed, so that one may look forward to their growing use.

I have dwelt overlong on this aspect of the matter simply to emphasize the fact that ideas which were only a gleam in the eye of the scientist ten years ago have in that period completely changed the field of contraceptive technology. Moreover, we are at the beginning, not at the end, of technological progress in this field. Thanks to the research support given in the past decade to the physiology of reproduction the prospects for new developments are extremely good. No one can be sure what precise form they will take, but experts in the field agree that within three or four years much more useful methods will be available.

One such possibility, on which the animal work is far advanced, involves an injection or an implant that will prevent pregnancy for a year or more. It is hoped to release a progestin in such very small amounts that its effect is achieved exclusively at the uterine level without involving either the ovary or the pituitary. If this proves to be possible, the reduction of dosage and the elimination of estrogens should greatly reduce the undesirable side effects of the present combined pill, and bring the costs well under 50 cents a year per patient. It remains to be seen whether this or other interesting ideas mature, but rapid progress in contraceptive technology seems highly probable. No other single development could mean as much in promoting the practice of birth control in the next decades. Weakly motivated populations require simple and convenient methods.

MOTIVATION

It is around the problem of motivations for the restriction of child-bearing in the Less-Developed Regions that the most serious questions arise. It is widely agreed that the motivation for restriction comes most rapidly in the context of urban-industrial development, improving health, popular education and the rising status of women. Low birth rates have on occasion occurred in the absence of these developments, but not very often. This fact has led to the view that the the response to efforts to spread birth control will be small. It is argued that illiterate peasants are most unlikely to be interested in such radically innovative behavior as contraceptive practice while they are under the influence of the strong familial institutions in societies where survival, not over-rapid growth, has been the agelong problem. In order to reach the conclusion that it is a waste of time to try to reduce birth rates, all these propositions are put forth along with the fact that a number of nations have talked about it without doing anything. This emphasis on lack of motivation comes out in sophisticated Communist discussions. Without social-economic development the birth rate will not come down; given proper development it will come down automatically. From this the inference is drawn that we should get on with development and stop wasting resources and personnel on family planning.

The same generally accepted theory that motives for restriction are more important than means is used to diametrically opposite ends by Professor Kingsley Davis (*Science,* 10 November, 1967). He thinks that the social situation is too unfavorable to stimulate the voluntary acceptance of family planning on a sufficient scale to bring substantial reductions in the rate of population growth. Therefore, he believes that new emphasis should be given to intensifying the motives for restriction, and only secondary importance should be attached to increasing the availability of the means for restriction. Governments should, he thinks, have policies that somewhat drastically reward restriction while penalizing early marriage and the large family. The Communists look to automatic changes; Davis looks to legal and administrative changes in incentives.

Others, including myself, are inclined to the view that in the Less-Developed Regions there is not now either the will or the ability to achieve governmental coercion, and that, in any case, attempts to foster innovative behavior by drastic governmental action would do more harm than good. In this type of situation the public can be more easily led than pushed. It is my personal impression that, for example, efforts to raise ages at marriage drastically while making abortion compulsory for the illegitimates, and sterilization compulsory after a specified number of births, would be more likely to bring down the government than the birth rate. The same basic attitudes that tend to slow the acceptance of voluntary family planning will constrain the governments from drastic coercion.

Of course, the reason for the somewhat sharp disagreements is that the matter cannot be proved one way or another beyond any chance of doubt. All parties can allude to general principles, neglect magnitudes and time scales, and weigh the evidence to draw conclusions to their taste.

For my part, I am convinced that very generally the underlying social-economic situation in most of the Less-Developed Regions has already changed in ways that have enhanced interest in the limitation of childbearing. I think that a very considerable speeding of the reduction of birth rates in the Less-Developed Regions can be achieved through the spread of voluntary family planning, and on a scale that matters. Moreover, I think it can be done without coercion and with a relatively small deployment of resources. Let us review some of the reasons for this conviction.

REASONS FOR OPTIMISM

Health—It is often argued that since surviving children provide the only parental guarantee of security, parents will be unwilling to limit their childbearing until death rates are much reduced. But in most of the Less-Developed Regions death rates have been drastically reduced. The populations are well aware of the fact that children now survive. Families, in the sense of surviving members, have become drastically larger. A few decades ago the families were not large in the traditional societies; indeed many were born but few survived. The families of survivors were much smaller than in the modern West. With the dramatic improvement in the control of contagious and infectious disease, families have indeed become large. Some restriction of childbearing under these new circumstances is required to bring the families back toward their more traditional size. It is my own experience that peasants, concerned with land for their children, have a lively appreciation of that fact. It is clear that children are highly valued the world around, but it is not clear that even the traditional societies require unlimited numbers. The improvement in health represents a major step in the process of modernization. It alone has increased the interest in restricting childbearing.

Public Interest—Statements of public interest in birth control do not have to rest on theory. There have been careful surveys in more than a score of countries. They show that, save among nomadic peoples, there is everywhere a substantial majority of women who want to limit their childbearing. This does not mean that they want only two children, but it does mean that they are interested in birth control. Objections are raised that the surveys are not perfectly done, that respondents aim to please, and that verbal responses are a far cry from action. All this is true, but it is also a fact that the internal differences shown by the surveys are systematic and in the direction suggested by prior theory. Furthermore, in South Korea and Taiwan where there are active governmental programs, the results from repeated surveys are shifting in the expected direction. In short, the results are reasonable and without exception they show between 60 and 80 per cent of the women professing an interest in contraceptive practice.

But verbal response to questionnaires is by no means the only evidence of interest. As we have seen, illegal abortion is rife in Latin America. It is also far from negligible in both Africa and Asia. It is difficult to argue that women who are willing to risk their lives and health by securing crude abortions have no interest in limiting the number of children.

Of course the main evidence of public interest is the fact that when reasonably good services are organized the women come for help in very large numbers. This is true whether it is in the rural areas of Thailand, the slums of Santiago, or the large maternity hospitals of major urban centers. The critics make much of the fact that in the initial stages of a program very often there is not a flood of patients. Unfortunately, in the early stages of a program the services are often appallingly inferior. There will not be a flood of patients if, after having walked miles to a clinic, they find doctors but no supplies, or supplies but no doctor, and on return are asked to come back tomorrow.

There has been a considerable tendency to announce the failure of the birth control programs in India and in Pakistan and to draw the inference that the trouble lay in the lack of public interest. Both countries have had the needed policies since before 1959, and neither can yet point with certainty to a reduction of the birth rates. The case is hardly fair. In fact, very little was done in either country until the IUD emerged. Since the major administrative reorganizations, we have had three or four years of seriously pushed programs. Unquestionably they leave much to be desired. It is not a simple matter to organize an efficient service in these huge countries which have great illiteracy, poverty, and religious, linguistic and community cleavages. Indeed, to do so presents many of the same problems as organizing a program of improved agricultural production.

Now the family planning programs of both countries appear to be moving. In India, more than 3.2 million sterilizations have been performed, and some two to three million IUDs have been inserted. In Pakistan, sterilizations are running about 10,000 a month and IUD insertions over 60,000 a month, and there is every expectation that these figures will rise. Pakistan by now may have cut a point or so off its birth rate. To call programs failures when they have been given vitality for only a few years seems unfortunate. However, it is a smaller error than to blame the inadequacy of the results on public apathy. The overwhelming fault lies in bureaucratic inefficiency; the failures are those of the professionals, not the peasants.

Encouraging Accomplishments—The clinching fact is that in smaller areas with active birth control programs the birth rates have been rapidly and consequentially reduced. This is the case in South Korea, Taiwan, Hong Kong and Singapore. In South Korea and in Taiwan, more than 25 per cent of the women of childbearing age are now either sterilized or practicing modern and highly effective contraception. There are no reliable birth rates for Korea, but many lines of evidence make it clear that the birth rate must be falling fast. In Taiwan, where the birth rate was well over 40 per 1,000 population in 1955, it is now well below 30. Similarly, low rates are found in Singapore and Hong Kong and are clearly related to the growing prevalence and effectiveness of contraceptive practice.

But the critics are hard to please. It is not sufficient to show that the family planning programs are attracting large numbers of patients, that the patients are practicing highly effective contraception, and that the birth rates are declining. Yes, they say, the birth rate is falling, but it was falling before the family planning programs were started. So they were, by about 2 per cent per year, but now they are falling by more than 3 per cent per year. "Yes, but" say the critics, the birth rate might well have fallen just as fast or even faster if there were no program. Perhaps then the age at marriage would have risen faster, and illegal abortion and sterilization might have increased more rapidly. This is, of course, possible. One cannot absolutely prove what might have happened under different circumstances. It is more than a little difficult, however, to understand how not helping people avoid pregnancy when they want to could foster a faster decline of the birth rate.

"Yes, but" say the critics, they use the IUD and sometimes the Pill, and the evidence is that half of the patients discontinue the use of these methods within two years, which is a small proportion of the childbearing period. This is true, but it is also true that most of those discontinuing do not return to the unprotected state. They shift to other methods, to abortion and to sterilization. The total history of the patients shows a consequentially reduced pregnancy rate.

The argument continues nonetheless. "Yes, but" say the critics, the women accepting help are for the most part old, and have already borne many children. Their future contribution would be small even if they took no precautions. Here Professor Robert G. Potter and his colleagues (*Science,* 24 May, 1968) have the answers. They show clearly that the older women coming for help are a self-selected, high-fertility part of their age group. Their further reproduction without protection would be highly significant.

"Yes, but" say the critics, these programs are merely skimming the cream of the highly motivated small minority in a society that is not really interested in birth control. In fact there is no evidence that the programs are running out of cream, either in South Korea or in Taiwan, although it is always possible that they will do so; clearly, one does start with the highly motivated. The encouraging fact is that in Taiwan, at least, as the program goes on the new patients have a lower average age and a smaller average number of children.

Much is made by the critics of the fact that the traditional values of the society influence reproductive behavior; too little is made of the fact that behavior influences the values of the society. One can, indeed, argue that the most rapid means of introducing family planning is to make the service readily available to the older women, the bearers of propriety, and those facing the most acute problems. It can be argued that nothing is likely to change the values more rapidly than the demonstration effect of an innovative leadership.

Almost certainly one cannot expect the nations of the Asian Mainland to be able to move as rapidly as South Korea, Taiwan, Hong Kong and Singapore. In all except South Korea the levels of prosperity and education are quite high, and social change is rapid. Korea is heavily illiterate and very poor but moving rapidly ahead. It is, however, a nation in which the years of conflict have done much to break the cake of ancient custom. It, too, is in a state of rapid change. But ten years ago, before the fact, how many of us would have said that these Oriental familistic populations were so ready for change that the success of their birth control programs would have no relevance for other parts of the world? To me, their experience suggests that energetic programs can indeed bring reasonably rapid results elsewhere.   **1470610**

The changes of the past decade are remarkably heartening, and they have come at a pace scarcely dreamed of a decade ago. It is not the shortcomings but the accomplishments that are surprising. We have strong governmental policies through most of Asia and parts of Africa and Latin America. We have demonstrated interest in family planning on the part of the majority of the public. We have contraceptive methods with hitherto undreamed-of efficiency, and still more appropriate methods in the offing. We have the fact that the governments of several small countries have shown that a strong program to spread family planning has brought consequential reductions of the birth rate in a relatively short time. The experience of the decade bodes well for the years ahead.

Less Controversy—Finally, there has been a clear reduction of the ideological and religious controversies. There is little difference in the interpretations of the demographic situations. The difference relates mainly to the unwillingness of the Communists and the Catholics to stress the importance of family planning. However, at least prior to the encyclical of July, 1968, banning all artificial means, neither the Catholics nor the Communists were openly opposing assistance for birth control by international organizations, provided such assistance is requested by the governments concerned and does not entail the coercion of the individual. These changes in position have eased the problems of international technical assistance and of national program formulations.

I think that the foregoing all adds up to the fact that the world's extremely dangerous problems of rapid population growth can be greatly reduced in the coming decades. Thus far, on a world-wide basis, nothing has really been done to reduce rates of population growth. But we have learned in the past decades that a world sufficiently interested to try energetically can speed the reduction of human fertility enough to make consequential reductions in the rate of population growth. We do not have the solution, but we do have the prerequisites for a solution in terms of policy, program, methods, public interest, and demonstrated results. Only the work remains to be done.

I can see nothing on the horizon that is likely to reverse these recent trends except the losses of a cataclysmic war, which we have ruled out by assumption. The Pope's refusal to yield to the modernizing forces within the Roman Church will probably retard matters a bit. Presumably it will be of little consequence in the Moslem, Hindu and Buddhist worlds. In the Catholic countries it is likely to have more influence on the "word" than on the "act." In Latin America it may block formal governmental involvement in family planning, and thereby give special importance to the kind of quasi-governmental activities that have in any case been developing. Otherwise all the technological, social, economic and political forces seem to be working toward an acceleration of the new trend toward family planning. The real question is what to expect under the circumstances.

The Prospects for Growth

Perhaps the foregoing is sufficient justification for my belief that the Medium projection of the U.N. as adjusted for Mainland East Asia is a sufficiently high alternative. It calls for a rapid decline of both mortality and fertility, without presupposing worldwide efforts to speed the decline of the birth rate. I am, therefore, content with the Adjusted U.N. Medium figure of a World Population of 6.7 billion for the year 2000 as a high figure.

But what of a low alternative? What if the move toward family planning gains great strength on a world-wide basis? It seems to me that the foregoing makes it amply clear that there simply is no scientific way of forecasting the result. About the best we can do is what the U.N. staff did; in effect, they simply cut the birth rate more drastically than they really thought would prove feasible.

Perhaps the recent work of Thomas Frejka will help with our judgment on this matter. This Czechoslovakian demographer has an interesting approach to the problem. He assumes that mortality will decline along much the same course as that projected by the

U.N. Then he asks what the world population will be by the end of the century, given various kinds of declines in the net reproduction rate. The net reproduction rate is the ratio of the daughter to the mother generation that would arise if the age schedules of female fertility and mortality were to remain fixed in a closed population. A net reproduction rate of 1.0 is required to maintain a stationary population. In 1960 the net reproduction rate for the world was estimated at about 1.66, which in the long run would produce a 66 per cent increase every generation of about 27 years. One of the assumptions that Frejka examines is that from 1965 on the net reproduction rate declines steadily, until by the end of the century it reaches 1.0, the level that generates a stationary population. This is truly a drastic drop. It requires the world average to fall in 35 years to a level that very few countries have sustained for any substantial period. It is hard for me to imagine a faster decline, but it is perhaps one that could be reached if world-wide preoccupation with slowing the rate of growth continues to grow stronger. It would not mean the end of population growth, which would continue for some decades into the next century until the age distribution settled down to that characteristic of the new structure of vital rates. But it would mean that the world had, in effect, solved its problems of population growth within this century. A world that is sufficiently concerned to cut its fertility to the level required for replacement under conditions of good health, could cope with its remaining problems of growth.

To me it seems an appealing minimum, but it implies by the year 2000 a world population of 5.6 billion. It is much the same as the U.N. Low projection, and about a half-billion below the Adjusted Low Projection.

So far as numbers go we can summarize the situation as follows: the world, which had about 3 billion people in 1960, may have as many as 6.7 billion by the end of the century, assuming as we have that population growth will be unconstrained by war or famine until the end of the century. If birth control practices are energetically fostered by governments and international agencies, particularly in the Less-Developed Regions, the population by the end of the century might be held to 6 billion or a little lower. In any case, it seems highly improbable that the population can be held to less than 5.5 billion. The difference between 6.7 billion and, say, 5.7 billion by the end of the century may be thought of as the reward for an energetic world-wide effort to reduce fertility.

The world which provided inadequate diets for a large proportion of its 3 billion people in 1960 faces the problem of feeding about twice that number by the year 2000, even if strenuous efforts are made to reduce birth rates. It might have to feed 3.7 billion more. Nor is that all of the difficulty. Only something like 400 million of the increase is projected for the More-Developed Regions. Between 1960 and the end of the century the Less-Developed Regions face, under the best of circumstances, a population growth that virtually equals that of the world today. Clearly it will be a heroic undertaking to absorb such increases while lifting the levels of nutrition.

The alternative may well be a massive loss of life generated by the breakdown of barriers to the spread of starvation and disease. This danger is greatly intensified by the ways in which the coming increase must be distributed between agricultural pursuits, non-agricultural pursuits, and mass unemployment. Past history suggests that the strongest efforts to lift agricultural product will make small demands for additional labor force. Since the labor force will be growing more rapidly than the population the expansion must come very rapidly either in nonagricultural pursuits or in unemployment; one is costly and the other intolerably dangerous in terms of political stability. Clearly the extremely rapid growth of urban population that we have witnessed in recent years will continue. The projection of total population is difficult, but the projections of future urban populations is almost impossible. Work on this problem is also going forward in the United Nations, but thus far only a working document subject to revision has resulted. In this study it is suggested that in each of several types of situations the rate of population growth for communities with 20,000 or more inhabitants has been about double the rate of growth of the total population. The preliminary work projects this situation into the future subject to the constraint that the number in rural areas and smaller cities not decline. On this kind of calculation, by the year 2000 the cities of the More-Developed Regions would have twice their 1960 populations, while the rural areas and small towns would remain stationary. In Less-Developed Regions rural and small city populations by 2000 would be 1.6 times the 1960 level. The city population would be 6.8 times as large as in 1960. On this projection the world population living in cities of 20,000 or more would quadruple in that forty year period. Obviously, no importance can be attached to these specific figures; they only serve to illustrate the fact that with modernization a disproportionate part of the population growth has gone to the cities, and will in all probability continue to do so. Finding the means for supporting this kind of increase outside of agriculture is no mean undertaking, but the alternative is intolerable mass unemployment.

To me, the moral of the story is clear. There is no realistic possibility that the control of human fertility can be a substitute for economic development. In the best terms the economic problems of the next decades are inevitably enormous if the world is to hold together. On the other hand, it is equally clear that energetic efforts to foster the limitation of fertility in the next four decades could reduce population growth by something between 700 million and possibly one billion. Clearly this would greatly simplify the problems of modernization and help reduce the risks of failure. The rewards would be very great. Unless fertility is reduced we shall enter the next century with growth potential unimpaired and shall face more doubling of larger populations. If fertility can be brought under control in this century, mankind may for the first time in its history have found the means of driving hunger and poverty from the earth.

Don Paarlberg

2

Food for More People
and Better Nutrition

This chapter will be concerned with projections of food production and needs, worldwide and by areas, to the year 2000.

Often, in speculation regarding the world food problem, the procedure is to project a certain carefully chosen rate of population growth and to extrapolate an enlightened estimate of the rate of increase in food production. Almost inevitably, the two projected rates will diverge, resulting in either a calculated deficit or a calculated surplus at the target date. The issue is posed as a race between food supply and population, with either "shortage" or "surplus" the overwhelming probability and "balance" a remote possibility. Food and population are treated as separate and independent variables, usually on "a collision course."

Such an approach is simplistic. It overlooks the enormous capacity for adjusting the use of agricultural resources and the food intake. In fact, the so-called race between food supply and population

Don Paarlberg *is Hillenbrand Professor of Agricultural Economics at Purdue University. He is a former United States Assistant Secretary of Agriculture and has written many articles dealing with agricultural policy and practices.*

41

invariably ends in a tie. If food is abundant, it is somehow concentrated and refined so as to fit into the existing number of human
stomachs. If food is scarce, the diet is changed so as to stretch the
supply to cover the need. If the limits of adjustment are reached
and there still is not enough food to go around, the human population is reduced proportionately.

The appropriate questions are: "How many people will there be
by the year 2000?" "How well will they be fed?" and, "What can
we do to improve nutritional levels?"

The wrong question is: "Will the world be able to feed its people by the year 2000?" Such people as are then in the world will be
fed; one cannot live on non-existent food. When the United Nations
projects a world population of 6,129 million ("medium variant")
by the year 2000, this is based on the necessary assumption that
there will be food for that many people.

Adjusters in the Food Supply

POTENTIALS FOR INCREASING FOOD

We understand rather well the concept of expanding food production by simply increasing total output from the present mix of
crops and livestock. This is, indeed, the procedure in most studies,
and it will be used prominently in this one. Not so well understood
are the potentials that come from *adjusting* the mix of inputs and
outputs. These will now be enumerated.

A big adjuster is livestock production. Professor Frank Pearson
of Cornell University tells us that it is possible to feed seven times
as many people on crops consumed directly as it is on crops first
consumed by livestock and converted into meat, milk and eggs to
be eaten by human beings. If the food supply is reduced, we eat the
livestock and then eat the crops the livestock otherwise would have
eaten. The potential of this adjuster is enormous. Not all countries
have this shock-absorber in their food supply. The United States
has it. We have a large livestock population. If we were willing to
accept a diet similar to that available to most people of the world,

we could easily feed several times our present population on the same acreage. Some countries, as in the Middle East, have long been so near the margin of want that the livestock population is very small and there is little cushion to avert disaster.

We must remember that downward adjustments in the diet—indeed, any abrupt change—will be strenuously resisted. Habit is strong and acquired tastes are powerful. People become accustomed to a particular diet and come to love it. Nature endowed the tongue with the function of tasting and conferred upon the digestive tract basic responsibility for nourishment. But the tongue, that notorious deceiver, was also given the gift of speech, while the digestive tract was left mute. So in most councils, whether knowingly or otherwise, taste and habits are more strongly represented than is nutrition. How much different our diets would be if taste were synonymous with nutrition, and if the tongue would correctly report both! The human organism has the capacity to derive acceptable nutrition from a wide range of foods. Note the great variation in the staples upon which various people rely: the Chinese with their rice, the Scots with their oatmeal, the Eskimo with his fish, the Arab with his fruit, the man of Punjab with his wheat, the Mexican with his corn and beans. Man is omnivorous, and in long-range food planning it is an error to treat him otherwise.

Intensification of cropping systems is a great adjuster in the food supply. In the United States, potatoes, rice and corn produce almost twice as many calories per acre as wheat, which we may take as a standard. Rye produces only half as much. Among the vegetables, carrots yield twice as much as wheat, while beets and celery yield about the same as wheat. Tomatoes, peas, lettuce, lima beans and asparagus yield only one-fifth to one-third as much as wheat. These ratios will vary from country to country and from year to year. The nutritive qualities of these different foods will also vary, of course. Gradually, over time, a cropping system emerges that takes into account agricultural resources, population density, food preferences, nutritive needs, and the state of technology. If food becomes more abundant, a country shifts away from the crops that produce large amounts of food; witness reduction in the acreage of potatoes and corn in the United States. If the population presses heavily on the food supply, the cropping system is intensified. Witness the high percentage of cropland in corn and potatoes in the Sierra region of Peru.

Technology is a great extender of the food supply. Spun protein, made from soybeans, provides a meat substitute nutritionally equivalent to hamburger, at about half the cost. Butterfat costs 70 cents a pound, while soybean oil is quoted at about 10 cents and can be made into an equally good spread. Food can be fortified with low-cost nutrients, natural or synthetic. Man-made fibers are replacing cotton and wool, releasing acreage for food production. As internal-combustion engines replace animal power, vast acreages are released from feed production for the production of human food. Synthetic sugar, at a fraction of the cost of natural sugar, supplies the sweetener for about 15 per cent of the soft-drink market. Algae, leaf protein, and single-cell protein produced from hydrocarbons are technically feasible sources of food, and in some cases may be economical as well, though they have severe handicaps of an aesthetic sort. Desalination of sea water may make possible irrigation and therefore food production in areas now barren. Food from the sea may increase, particularly with the development of fish protein concentrate. Some of these new developments may catch on; some may not. Few of them were discernible 30 years ago; who will defend the projection of present technology for the 30 years between now and the turn of the century?

Stocks of food are important adjusters. They are useful in the short run but can have little significance with regard to the problem here under consideration—the relationship of food to people by the year 2000. Stocks are more of a shock-absorber than a long-run adjuster.

Trade, of course, is a very potent adjuster, both in the short run and in the long run. If one part of the world has comparative advantage in agriculture and some other part has comparative advantage in industrial production, exports can adjust the food supply to the population in both areas, in a mutually helpful manner.

We have, then, these adjusters in the food supply: increased production, livestock farming, intensification of the cropping system, technology, stocks of food, and trade. How much flexibility do they provide? Enough so that during the recent disastrous crop years in India, said to be the worst in a century, widespread famine was averted. Enough so that Western Europe was able to avoid mass starvation during World War II, despite the fact that her food imports were largely cut off and that much of her agricultural production goods and many of her farm people were diverted to war. There is enough flexibility in these adjusters for the United States to upgrade the diet sharply during the past quarter century from a reduced acreage. There is enough flexibility in the system so that any projection of existing production patterns, existing diets, and existing rates of population growth, with the inevitable prediction of food gap or food surplus, is bound to be wrong.

But if disaster strikes and the adjusters are taxed beyond their maximum flexibility, hunger and starvation result. The society makes as many adjustments as possible on the food side of the equation. But the equation must be balanced, and if it cannot be balanced from the food side, it is balanced from the people side.

By what means do these adjustments occur? How is the need for adjustment communicated, back and forth, between those who produce food and those who consume it?

In the traditional subsistence economy the producer and the consumer are the same person, so that communication is easy. The subsistence farmer knows that he gets more food if he consumes his corn directly, rather than first feeding it to animals. And he acts readily in accordance with this knowledge.

In the market economy adjustments occur largely through price change. A high price signals the producer to supply additional output, and tells the consumer to turn to alternative foods. A low price persuades the consumer to use large amounts of the product in question, and informs the supplier to shift his resources to the production of other goods.

In a centrally directed economy these adjustments must be

brought about by edict. Those who are responsible for food policy must know the principles of food economics, they must have current information as to supplies and consumption, and they must have the political power to require adjustment.

The principles of economy in the production and use of foods are universal and the need for adjustment is continual. But the institutional setting within which adjustment occurs will vary radically from one country to another.

"Food requirement" is not a good phrase because it wrongly connotes that specificity and inflexibility are the dominant attributes of the diet. "Food supply" is likewise a slippery concept, whether measured in index numbers, or in quantities of specific crops, or in dollar values, or in total tons, or in pounds of dry matter, or in calories, or in some mix of stated nutrients; this phrase, too, conveys a deceptive rigidity. Depending on the circumstances, corn may be a human food, a beverage, an animal feed, or an industrial crop.

But, to get on with the task, some simplifying assumptions are needed. The important thing is that we do not let these assumptions take on the attributes of reality.

How Hungry Are the World's People?

THE NUTRITIONAL SITUATION

Before we project the need for food to the year 2000, it would be appropriate to take account of the nutritional situation as recently reported.

The National Advisory Commission on Food and Fiber reports[1] that the one billion people in the developed countries have half again as many calories and five times as much high-quality animal protein per person as the two billion people in the less-developed countries (1959–61):

[1] *Food and Fiber for the Future,* Report of the National Advisory Commission on Food and Fiber (Washington, D.C.: Superintendent of Documents, U.S. Government Printing Office, 1967), p. 308.

	Developed Countries	Underdeveloped Countries
Calories per person, daily	2,941	2,033
Total protein per person, daily grams	84.0	52.4
Animal protein only, per person, daily grams	38.8	7.2
Population in millions	1,089	1,923

The lesser body weight of people in many of the less-developed countries (in part a genetic difference) slightly mitigates the disadvantage shown in the table. Differing physical activity is another variable. But even after accounting for these factors, the differences are still marked.

There is in these figures, of course, the deceptiveness latent in all averages. Though on the average there may be sufficient food, some individuals in the society may be in dire need. It is possible for a man to drown in a stream that averages only 18 inches deep.

Even in the United States, where food supplies are on the whole abundant, there are instances of hunger and malnutrition. How frequent these instances are, and the causes of them, are matters of dispute. About six million people in the United States are participating in family food assistance programs. The oldest of these programs is direct distribution of government-owned food to people certified by state and local officials as needy. In fiscal 1968, 3,600,000 people from 1,384 areas participated in this program, receiving a part of their food needs. The cost of this program in fiscal 1967 was $101 million. Some sixteen different commodities are distributed. Some of the donated commodities are acquired through price support operations, some are purchased to bolster farm prices, and some are bought to round out the nutritional needs of the recipients. The program is cooperative as between the federal government, the states, and the local areas.

Since 1961 the emphasis in our domestic food subsidy programs has been on the Food Stamp Program. In fiscal year 1968 there were

2,500,000 people from 1,027 areas participating in the program at a cost of approximately $185 million. The program is being expanded and is intended eventually to be offered to virtually all of the people on relief.

Eligible for participation in the Food Stamp Program are people who have been certified by local officials as being in need, usually those on relief. Standards are set up, based on the number of dollars required to buy a nutritionally adequate, low-cost diet. To make possible the purchase of such a diet the qualified people pay money and receive stamps.

How much do they pay? If their incomes are very low the payment is nominal. If their incomes are higher, near what is called the cut-off point, they pay much more. On the average, they pay $6 for stamps that will buy $10 worth of food. This food they buy in the grocery stores, passing down the aisles with their grocery carts, indistinguishable from the other patrons. The difference is that they use food stamps instead of bank notes at the checkout counter.

About 20 million school children are now participating daily in the School Lunch Program. The cost of a lunch today averages between 50 and 55 cents, for which the average charge per child is about 28 cents. The difference is made up by federal, state and local funds. The Special School Milk Program operates like the School Lunch Program, milk being its particular focus. In fiscal 1968 the estimated federal cost of the Special School Milk Program was $104 million and the cost of the School Lunch Program was $222 million.

If adequate nutrition is a problem of some dimensions in the affluent United States, it is clear that the problem must be enormously greater in the less-developed countries. The President's Science Advisory Committee reports:

> Isolated results, published since 1952, suggest that the prevalence of kwashiorkor (protein malnutrition) and marasmus (calorie malnutrition) ranges from one to more than 10 per cent in pre-school children of developing countries. Criteria for identifying these extreme deficiency states have been established only recently, however, and the extremely high mortality rates in the 1 to 4 year age group in develop-

ing countries suggest that moderate protein-calorie malnutrition affects
at least 50 per cent of these children.

Anemia, goiter, xerophthalmia, pellagra, beriberi, rickets and other
diseases associated with malnutrition are to be found in great or less
degree in various parts of the world. In 1963 the Third World Food
Survey was conducted by the Food and Agriculture Organization
of the United Nations as part of its Freedom from Hunger campaign. According to the survey, at least 20 per cent of the population
of the less-developed countries was undernourished and some 60 per
cent received diets inadequate in nutritional quality.

The President's Science Advisory Committee thus generalizes the
inadequacy in nutrition among the people in the less-developed
countries of the world: "A sustained improvement in the nutrition
of children in poor countries can be expected to increase the average body weight of adults 10 per cent or more during the next two
decades, with a corresponding increase in food needs."

In popular literature there are frequent references to the numbers of people who "go to bed hungry." Sometimes this is said to
be one-third of the world's population, sometimes half. There is
no way to verify or refute these statements. So far as is known,
there has been no world-wide Gallup Poll, interrogating bedgoing
people on this point. (Parenthetically, it is not clear why the trag-
edy of hunger should be more dramatic at bedtime than at other
hours during the day.)

Even where the per capita food supply is low, hunger usually is
not continual. It tends to occur during the period when last year's
stocks are depleted and before the new crop comes in. During other
parts of the year hunger may not be prevalent. Just as the deer and
the bird have their season of critically low food supply and live reasonably well at other times of the year, so it is with man.

There are no reliable figures on the number of people who die
of starvation. The reasons for this are understandable. Hunger and
malnutrition weaken the body and lower the resistance to a wide
range of diseases. When death occurs, the hunger-induced disease
may be listed as the cause. National pride is a factor in suppressing

the fact of starvation. Much of the real hunger in the world is be-
yond the range of the statisticians. But hunger is as old as history.
G. I. Burch reported in a bulletin of the Population Reference Bu-
reau that between 10 and 1846 A.D. there were 201 famines in the
British Isles. A study of Nanking University reported that from 108
B.C. to 1911 A.D. there were 1,828 famines in China.

In fact, our age is unique in the rarity of famine. There have
been deaths from hunger, often as a result of revolution or political
disturbance, as in Communist China in the early 'sixties and, more
recently, in Biafra. On the other hand, there have been politically
averted famines as during the Indian crop failure of 1966, when
the United States supplied that country with wheat on a concessionary basis. There has been no major famine in the world since the
Bengal famine of 1948. There is no known previous famine-free period of equal length. The present is not a time for despair. Ours is
the first generation to dare to think in terms of food enough for all.
In this respect ours is a time for hope.

Hunger is not new. The new thing is our awareness of it, our
concern about it, and our intention to help alleviate it.

TRENDS IN FOOD PRODUCTION

As a prelude to projections of food production and needs to the
beginning of the twenty-first century, it would be good to learn
whether we have been gaining or slipping back in recent years.
Data, in the form of index numbers, are provided by the U.S. Department of Agriculture (Table 1). The picture that emerges is that
when averages are taken, food production has kept ahead of population growth, both in the developed and the less-developed countries. The average man in the less-developed countries of the world,
though poorly nourished by any accepted standard, eats slightly better than did his father or his grandfather.

But one should not take great comfort from the slight overall
improvement that has occurred. There are large areas in which the
food situation, formerly poor, has in fact deteriorated. The Department of Agriculture reports that in the Caribbean area per capita
food production in 1967 stood at an index of 76, with 1957–59 equal

TABLE 1. *World Agricultural Production, Total and Per Capita, 1960–67*
(1957–59 = 100)

Area	1960	1961	1962	1963	1964	1965	1966	1967[1]
	Total							
World (excluding communist Asia)	106	108	111	114	117	118	122	127
Developed countries[2]	106	107	111	112	116	117	123	126
Less-developed countries[3]	107	111	112	117	119	121	120	130
India	110	115	110	117	120	109	107	128
Other less-developed countries	106	109	113	117	119	126	125	130
	Per capita							
World (excluding communist Asia)	102	102	103	103	104	103	104	107
Developed countries[2]	103	103	106	105	108	107	112	113
Less-developed countries[3]	102	103	102	103	103	102	98	104
India	105	108	101	104	105	93	89	104
Other less-developed countries	101	101	102	103	102	105	102	103

[1] Preliminary.

[2] North America, Europe, USSR, Japan, Republic of South Africa, Australia and New Zealand.

[3] Latin America, Asia (except Japan and communist Asia) and Africa (except Republic of South Africa).

Source: *The World Agricultural Situation, Review of 1967 and Outlook for 1968*, Foreign Agricultural Economic Report No. 38, U.S. Department of Agriculture, Washington, D.C., February 20, 1968, p. 6.

to 100. In 15 of the 37 African and West Asian countries for which statistics are available, per capita agricultural production declined from 1957–59 to 1967. Furthermore, the citizen of the less-developed country is not interested in comparing his food supply with that of his father; with his new awareness of the world about him he compares his food supply with that of his well-fed neighbor or with some new standard toward which he strives.

Requirements to the Year 2000

Thorkil Kristensen, Secretary-General of the Organization for Economic Cooperation and Development, has published preliminary findings of a study of the world food problem undertaken in conjunction with the Food and Agriculture Organization of the United Nations. The target date for his study is the year 2000. His paper was given on August 23, 1967, at the Thirteenth Conference of the International Association of Agricultural Economists at Sydney, Australia. Dr. Kristensen dealt with the non-communist world only, and concerned himself with both food supplies and the demand for food. His figures are expressed in American dollars of constant purchasing power; this permits him to aggregate various foods at their market value. His assumptions are explicit. His assumed growth rates for demand are based on:

1. United Nations population projections (high variant for developed countries 1960–2000 and for the less-developed countries 1960–70, medium variant for less-developed countries 1970–2000). Dr. Kristensen's population projections are therefore similar to those used by Professor Notestein in Chapter 1 of this book.
2. Growth of Gross Domestic Product (value of total production of goods and services) as in recent years with some progressive slowing down in developed countries and some speeding up in less-developed countries on the average; and
3. Income elasticities as estimated by the Food and Agriculture Organization with the assumption that in the less-developed countries total private consumption will increase more slowly than Gross Domestic Product because the rate of investment must be increased.

Concerning food production, Dr. Kristensen's assumptions are:

1. For the developed countries, the 1960–80 rate corresponds to actual growth during 1955–65.
2. For the less-developed countries, the rate for 1960–80 is slightly higher than actual performance 1955–65.
3. For the years 1980–2000 a slowing down is foreseen for the developed countries, while at the same time a faster rate of growth is assumed for the less-developed countries.

TABLE 2. *Demand, Production and Trade in Food in the Developed and the Less-Developed Countries of the Non-Communist World, 1960, 1980, and 2000, in Billions of Constant U. S. Dollars.*

	Total (billions of dollars)					
	Developed countries			Less-developed countries		
	1960	1980	2000	1960	1980	2000
Demand	80	113	151	47	89	170
Production	78	125	186	48	77	135
	−2	+12	+35	+1	−12	−35

	Annual Increase (per cent)			
	1960–1980	1980–2000	1960–1980	1980–2000
Demand	1.75	1.5	3.25	3.3
Production	2.4	2.0	2.4	−2.8

Source: Thorkil Kristensen, "The Approaches and Findings of Economists," *International Journal of Agrarian Affairs*, Vol. V, No. 2, Oxford University Press, London, May 1967, p. 139.

PROJECTED BALANCES

Dr. Kristensen projects a balance between the production of food and the demand for food, taking the non-communist world as a whole. His assumptions have been chosen so as to force this balance. But, on the basis of his projections, the balance would be achieved by a massive and growing transfer of food from the developed to the less-developed countries. Dr. Kristensen's projections would permit some modest improvement in the average diet; the slowly rising per capita Gross National Product would make it possible for people to buy slightly more and better food. And he assumes that advancing technology would get the extra food produced. Dr. Kristensen's work is concerned with projections, which are not considered to be predictions. Rather, they are intended to reveal the magnitude of the challenge ahead. It is indeed difficult to see how, by the year 2000, the less-developed countries, in the aggregate, would be able to

generate the foreign exchange with which to import 20 per cent of
their food needs. And it is hard to see a food donation program of
such magnitude.

The pioneering work that first focused the attention of the American people on the world food problem was a 1963 publication of the
Department of Agriculture titled *Man, Land and Food,* under the
authorship of Lester R. Brown. Brown's and Kristensen's general
views of the world food problem are similar. This publication cen-
tered on cereal grains, which constitute the backbone of the world
food supply. It projected grain production and utilization to the
year 2000, and offered two models, Model I maintaining current
consumption levels in the less-developed world, and Model II achieving modest consumption gains. The entire world, free and centrally
directed, was included in the study. World population numbers for
the year 2000 were set at 6.3 billion, the medium variant of the 1958
projections made by the United Nations. This is near the middle of
the range projected by Professor Notestein in Chapter 1.

While much has happened since the Department of Agriculture's
estimates were made, they are still reasonably indicative of the
basic situation. They are therefore presented at this point.

Table 3 indicates, on a per capita basis, the amount of grain that

TABLE 3. *Model I: Per Capita Annual Grain Production, Net Trade, and Availability,
by Regions, 1957/58–1960/61 and Projections to 2000 (in kilograms).*[1]

	1957/58–1960/61	2000
Geographic regions		
North America		
Production	1,057	1,200
Net trade	−174	−300
Availability	883	900
Latin America		
Production	211	196
Net trade	−4	+11
Availability	207	207
Western Europe		
Production	286	420
Net trade	+78	+80
Availability	364	500

TABLE 3. *Continued*

	1957/58–1960/61	2000
Eastern Europe and USSR		
Production	541	617
Net trade	+1	+8
Availability	542	625
Africa		
Production	165	159
Net trade	+6	+12
Availability	171	171
Asia		
Production	223	216
Net trade	+7	+14
Availability	230	230
Oceania		
Production	533	710
Net trade	−239	−400
Availability	294	310
Economic regions		
Developed regions		
Production	568	696
Net trade	−18	−53
Availability	550	643
Less-developed regions		
Production	215	208
Net trade	+7	+14
Availability	222	222
Political regions		
Free World		
Production	306	295
Net trade	−2	−5
Availability	304	290
Communist Bloc[2]		
Production	345	334
Net trade	+3	+9
Availability	348	343

[1] Plus sign = net imports; minus sign = net exports.
[2] Cuba not included.

Source: Lester R. Brown, *Man, Land and Food*, Foreign Agricultural Economic Report No. 11, Economic Research Service, U.S. Department of Agriculture, Washington, D.C., November 1963, p. 119.

would have to be available, either through production or trade, to hold per capita food supplies in the less-developed countries at the levels that have recently prevailed. The table reveals that the average North American has about four times as much grain available as the average person in the less-developed countries. The difference is that the North Americans feed much of it to livestock while the people of the less-developed countries consume it directly.

To achieve the per capita production required to maintain diets in the less-developed countries at their present levels, output would have to increase as shown in Table 4. The figures are not so much

TABLE 4. *Model I: Total Annual Grain Production, Net Trade, and Availability, by Regions, 1957/58–1960/61 and Projections to 2000 (in million metric tons).*[1]

	1957/58–1960/61	2000
Geographic regions		
North America		
Production	204	375
Net trade	−34	−94
Availability	170	281
Latin America		
Production	42	116
Net trade	−1	+7
Availability	41	123
Western Europe		
Production	85	176
Net trade	+23	+34
Availability	108	210
Eastern Europe and USSR		
Production	180	325
Net trade	2	+4
Availability	180	329
Africa		
Production	38	82
Net trade	+1	+6
Availability	39	88
Asia		
Production	353	836
Net trade	+12	+54
Availability	365	890

TABLE 4. *Continued*

	1957/58–1960/61	2000
Oceania		
Production	8	21
Net trade	−4	−12
Availability	4	9
Economic regions		
Developed regions		
Production	476	897
Net trade[3]	−15	−68
Availability	461	829
Less-developed regions		
Production	433	1,034
Net trade[3]	+15	+68
Availability	448	1,102
Political regions		
Free World		
Production	574	1,232
Net trade[3]	−3	−19
Availability	571	1,213
Communist Bloc[4]		
Production	336	698
Net trade[3]	+3[5]	+19
Availability	339	717

[1] Plus sign = net imports; minus sign = net exports.

[2] Negative but less than 500,000 metric tons.

[3] Net trade for economic regions may not equal total of geographic regions due to rounding.

[4] Cuba not included.

[5] Although complete data on net trade for the Bloc countries are not available for this period, net imports are assumed equal to the net exports of the Free World.

Source: Lester R. Brown, *Man, Land and Food*, Foreign Agricultural Economic Report No. 11, Economic Research Service, U.S. Department of Agriculture, Washington, D.C., November 1963, p. 120.

a prediction of what will occur as they are an effort to show what must happen if diets are not to deteriorate. In the less-developed regions, grain production would have to increase almost two and a half times in 40 years.

But the concern about food in the less-developed countries will not be satisfied if per capita food availability merely holds its own. Hunger and malnutrition are a fact. These people are increasingly aware of their hunger and their poverty. They are experiencing a revolution of rising expectations. They insist that life be better for them, or, if not for them, then certainly for their children. The day may be approaching of which Edwin Markham asked:

> How will the Future reckon with this man?
> How answer his brute questions in that hour
> When whirlwinds of rebellion shake all shores?

Table 5 projects a 10 per cent increase in per capita availability of grain between 1960 and 1980, and another 10 per cent increase

TABLE 5. *Model II: Per Capita Annual Grain Production, Net Trade, and Availability, by Regions, 1957/58–1960/61 and Projections to 2000 (in kilograms).*[1]

	1957/58–1960/61	2000
Geographic regions		
North America		
Production	1,057	1,200
Net trade	−174	−300
Availability	883	900
Latin America		
Production	211	237
Net trade	−4	+11
Availability	207	248
Western Europe		
Production	286	420
Net trade	+78	+80
Availability	364	500
Eastern Europe and USSR		
Production	541	617
Net trade	+1	+8
Availability	542	625
Africa		
Production	165	193
Net trade	+6	+12
Availability	171	205

TABLE 5. *Continued*

	1957/58–1960/61	2000
Asia		
Production	223	262
Net trade	+7	+14
Availability	230	276
Oceania		
Production	533	710
Net trade	−239	−400
Availability	294	310
Economic regions		
Developed regions		
Production	568	697
Net trade	−18	−53
Availability	550	644
Less-developed regions		
Production	215	251
Net trade	+7	+14
Availability	222	265
Political regions		
Free World		
Production	306	329
Net trade	−2	−5
Availability	304	324
Communist Bloc		
Production	345	371
Net trade	+3	+9
Availability	348	380

[1] Plus sign = net imports; minus sign = net exports.

Source: Lester R. Brown, *Man, Land and Food*, Foreign Agricultural Economic Report No. 11, Economic Research Service, U.S. Department of Agriculture, Washington, D.C., November 1963, p. 123.

by the year 2000. If half of the increased grain availability in the less-developed countries were converted to animal production, the gain in livestock product consumption would be about seven pounds per person, a modest increase indeed, gradually achieved over a period of 40 years.

TABLE 6. *Model II: Total Annual Grain Production, Net Trade, and Availability, by Regions, 1957/58–1960/61 and Projections to 2000 (in million metric tons).*[1]

	1957/58–1960/61	2000
Geographic regions		
North America		
Production	204	375
Net trade	−34	−94
Availability	170	281
Latin America		
Production	42	140
Net trade	−1	+7
Availability	41	147
Western Europe		
Production	85	176
Net trade	+23	+34
Availability	108	210
Eastern Europe and USSR		
Production	180	325
Net trade	2	+4
Availability	180	329
Africa		
Production	38	100
Net trade	+1	+6
Availability	39	106
Asia		
Production	353	1,014
Net trade	+12	+54
Availability	365	1,068
Oceania		
Production	8	21
Net trade	−4	−12
Availability	4	9
Economic regions		
Developed regions		
Production	476	897
Net trade[3]	−15	−68
Availability	461	829
Less-developed regions		
Production	433	1,253
Net trade[3]	+15	+68
Availability	448	1,321

TABLE 6. *Continued*

	1957/58–1960/61	2000
Political regions		
Free World		
Production	574	1,374
Net trade	−3	−19
Availability	571	1,355
Communist Bloc[4]		
Production	336	776
Net trade	+3[5]	+19
Availability	339	795

[1] Plus sign = net imports; minus sign = net exports.
[2] Negative but less than 500,000 metric tons.
[3] Net trade for economic regions may not equal total of geographic regions due to rounding.
[4] Cuba not included.
[5] Although complete data on net trade for the Bloc countries are not available for this period, net imports are assumed equal to the net exports of the Free World.

Source: Lester R. Brown, *Man, Land and Food*, Foreign Agricultural Economic Report No. 11, Economic Research Service, U.S. Department of Agriculture, Washington, D.C., November 1963, p. 124.

Table 6 shows the increase in grain production required to obtain this small improvement in the diet. In Latin America, for example, grain production would have to increase to three times the 1960 level, and, in addition, enormous imports would be necessary. The magnitude of the transfer of cereal grains from the developed to the less-developed countries is perhaps the most striking result of these projections. Expansion by a factor of 4 or 5 would be required.

The studies are more clearly an estimate of need than a prediction of the supplies that will be forthcoming. In fact, the procedures have generally been to estimate need based on certain criteria and then to compute the volume of production required to meet this need. Commonly, those who read these projections impute to them greater reliability than do those who make the analyses.

PRODUCTION VS. REPRODUCTION

These studies run to the year 2000, which is farther ahead than one can see with any assurance. As that date is approached, the economic visibility becomes very low indeed. But one thing is clearly revealed: Unless the present rate of population growth is checked, there is no solution to the world food problem. Projected beyond the turn of the century, present rates of population growth (and hence food needs) yield astronomical results. The only way in which it makes sense to talk about solving the world food problem is to envision and achieve some degree of control over population numbers.

Even if birth rates could be reduced sharply and soon (which is highly unlikely), the need for food in the world would continue to increase rapidly for a considerable number of years. In the less-developed countries of the world, 40 per cent of the people are 14 years of age or younger. These children, already in existence, will increase their per capita food intake as they progress toward adulthood. Modern medicine will continue to prolong the lives of those now living. And many new children will be born, even if birth rates are reduced.

The challenge to the world's agriculture is a great one, however measured. In the next section we consider agriculture's capability to meet this challenge.

Production Potentials Viewed

Projecting agricultural output is a hazardous undertaking. It would be far safer if it could be done on special paper, chemically treated so it would suddenly disintegrate at the end of five years.

One approaches this subject with proper humility if he recalls the various appraisals of food production within our own country, during times within memory. During the 1930's the prevailing diagnosis was for excess production. During the post-war population increase of the 1940's, the Department of Agriculture worried about our ability to supply the food for "the fifth plate." During the

1950's concern for surpluses again arose; this has been the prevailing appraisal except for a brief interlude during the middle 1960's, when it was thought that American agriculture should and would take on the job of feeding the world and would be strained to the utmost in this undertaking. These changing moods are more evident in the headlines than they are in the statistics. As a people, we prefer drama and variety in our assessment of public problems. If some fragment of evidence suggests a change, we are often quite ready to embrace it.

IN ADVANCED NATIONS

At various places in this book we refer to the developed nations. As commonly delineated, these are: the United States, Canada, Europe, U.S.S.R., Japan, Republic of South Africa, Australia, and New Zealand. All other nations are in the "less-developed" category.

What are the production potentials in the advanced nations? No qualified student seriously questions the capability of these countries, as a group, during the remainder of this century, to simultaneously:

1. Meet the challenge of population growth within their own borders,
2. Upgrade their own diets, and
3. Make available large and growing amounts of food for the less-developed countries.

The agricultural revolution, which is cumulative and irreversible, is far advanced in all of these developed countries. But it certainly has not run its course. There are good practices in use on some farms though not yet on others. There are advanced practises, now in the test plot, not yet in use on any farm. There are good ideas in the minds of researchers, ideas not yet tested. And there are trained new researchers, steadily increasing in number and skill, who will generate ideas that no one can yet foresee.

The rapid increase in crop yields in the developed countries (and the contrast with experience in the less-developed countries) is dramatically shown in Table 7. In North America crop yields have in-

TABLE 7. *Trends in Grain Yield Per Acre by Geographic and Economic Regions,*
1934–38 to 1960.

	Grain output per harvested acre (kilograms)		Per cent of increase 1934–38 to 1960	Per cent of annual compound rate of increase 1934–38 to 1960
	1934–38	1960		
Geographic regions				
North America	443	927	109	3.1
Latin America	461	498	8	.3
Western Europe	638	876	37	1.3
Eastern Europe and USSR	429	514	20	.8
Africa	265	318	20	.8
Asia	508	542	7	.3
Oceania	331	535	62	2.1
Economic regions[1]				
Developed regions	462	699	51	1.7
Less-developed regions	468	506	8	.3

[1] Less-developed regions are Asia, Africa, and Latin America; the remaining four regions are classified as developed.

Source: Lester R. Brown, *Increasing World Food Output*, Foreign Agricultural Economic Report No. 25, Economic Research Service, U.S. Department of Agriculture, Washington, D.C., April 1965, p. 61.

creased at a rate of more than 3 per cent, compounded annually, during the last quarter century. In Asia the annual rate of increase has been three-tenths of one per cent.

A common error is to think of the agricultural revolution as a transition from a low production plateau to a higher one. It is sometimes thought that the developed countries, having embarked on this transition quite some years ago, must now have nearly accomplished the change. Thus it is thought that production will soon level off, population will catch up, and problems of shortage will replace problems of plenty, even in the developed countries. This diagnosis had some supporters among professional agricultural economists until about a decade ago, when the reality of the agricultural revolution as a continuing phenomenon became clear to most students of the subject. Presently, the view of looming food shortage in the developed parts of the world is supported mainly by administrators who want additional appropriations for agricultural research, by proponents of local reclamation projects, by purveyors of farm supplies, by sellers of farm land, and by politicians who wish to engender hope for higher prices among their farmer constituents. Pockets of hunger and malnutrition in the developed parts of the world are primarily a matter of distribution and constitute a problem of a different sort.

The residual form in which the productive capacity of the developed countries is expressed is in the quantity of food available for export after supplying a better diet to the larger numbers of their own people. Three of the best analyses are those produced by the Food and Agriculture Organization, the Department of Agriculture, and the President's Science Advisory Committee. All of these show rapid growth in export capability. The President's Science Advisory Committee shows this capability as doubling between 1960 and 1980. The USDA would double this capability between 1960 and 1980 and double it again by the year 2000. The FAO essentially agrees with these projections.

These projections all envision the continuation of some restraints on agricultural output in the United States, which is the only one of the developed countries making a major effort to reduce production.

A word of caution must here be injected, a point that will be expanded later in the chapter: The capacity of the developed countries to provide food to the less-developed countries does not, in and of itself, constitute a solution to the world food problem. This is true for a number of reasons, of which only one will be stated at this point: Our capacity is small relative to the need. According to the above-cited USDA publication *Man, Land and Food,* page 120, the need for cereal grain in the less-developed countries by the year 2000 will increase by approximately 650 million metric tons from the 1960 figure, assuming no improvement in diets. The projected increase in the availability of grain for export from the developed countries is only 53 million tons. This comes out to only 8 per cent of the needed increase. Clearly, the developed countries can help some, but they cannot solve the problem on their own. The only place the problem can be solved is in the less-developed countries themselves.

IN LESS-DEVELOPED COUNTRIES

In India yields per acre average only about one-third as high as in Japan, although India on the whole is well favored with agricultural resources. In Turkey wheat is threshed by treading it out with oxen, as in Biblical times. In Malaya farmers are reluctant to use modern harvesting equipment, for fear of offending the rice spirit. In Nepal food is transported on the backs of men; people starve in the remote areas when crop failures occur. In Africa large areas are unfit for farming because of the tse-tse fly. In the high Andes of Peru the agricultural institutions are essentially feudal, similar to the system brought in by the Spaniards 350 years ago.

Yet in all these areas change is occurring. The agricultural revolution is not confined to the United States. It is proceeding everywhere, by different rates, from different levels. Evidence in support of this statement is that during the post-war period and up to now, with some outside help, the agriculture of the less-developed nations has, on the whole, kept up or more than kept up with rapid population growth.

Here and there spectacular advances have occurred. The example of Taiwan is instructive. Taiwan was in virtual chaos in the late 1940's. The island was small, hilly, heavily populated, torn by war and required to absorb a wave of migration from the mainland. But the people were sturdy, resolute, disciplined, fairly well educated, willing to accept a low level of living so that they could save and build up the economy. And they were willing to accept help. The United States helped, as did some other countries. But the major effort was by the Taiwanese themselves. American aid was terminated in 1965. Briefly, here is the record of achievement:

The Gross National Product increased, in real terms, by an average of more than 7 per cent per year for ten years.

Farm production has risen at a yearly rate of nearly 4.5 per cent. Yields per acre have almost doubled since 1950.

Industrial production increased about 13 per cent annually from 1952 to 1966.

Per capita income has increased, in real terms, at a rate of more than 3.5 per cent per year.

Total exports in 1967 were more than half a billion dollars, almost six times what they were in 1952.

Taiwan is now providing "second generation" technical assistance in food production to 19 African and two Asian countries. Six hundred technicians are engaged in such technical assistance and expenditures are almost $4 million.

In other places (for example, in some of the Caribbean countries) very little progress has been made. In some cases retrogression has occurred. Despite good soil and climate, agricultural development has not taken hold. Apathy and resignation seem to be the prevailing attitudes. American technical assistance seemingly has gone down the drain.

How can one estimate the production potential of such diverse countries? The problem is not limited to agricultural resources, as Bell, Hardin and Hill tell us in Chapter 4. Economic development in a larger sense is involved, together with problems that are institutional, social, political and psychological as well as agricultural. This Gunnar Myrdal tells us in his new book, *Asian Drama*.

There is some speculation about the possibility of a breakthrough in food production by opening up new land, particularly in South America and Africa, or by irrigating dry land, or by supplemental irrigation on land already used. In the long run substantial additional food might thus be produced. The President's Science Advisory Committee estimates that the potential for increase in irrigated area in the Indian subcontinent and Southeast and Southwest Asia is over 200 million acres. The total capital costs to develop irrigation in these areas would be approximately $80 billion. In

Latin America and Africa the limiting factors are not land and water but economic, institutional and social problems. To develop agriculture in many of these regions would take large-scale intercontinental migration. Such great changes would come about gradually and would yield their maximum results after the target date of our study. Most of the food used in the year 2000 will be produced on lands presently in use.

There are a number of quick simplistic answers to the world food problem. These have some plausibility and even some degree of truth. Most of them place the problem conveniently outside the range of American concern, help, or responsibility. Here are several:

"India could solve its food problem if the people would just kill off their sacred cows." The cows do compete to some degree with human beings for a limited food supply. But they also provide draft power, milk, fertilizer, and companionship. People do not ordinarily deify animals that worsen the human condition.

"If these people would work hard, like Americans, they wouldn't have any food problem." Given their food intake, their felt needs, and the marginal product of their labor, they probably work reasonably hard.

"There is enough food but the monkeys and the birds and the rats and weevils get it." Often true! The World Health Organization estimates that 20 per cent of the crops planted by man every year is eaten or spoiled by rodents and insects even before harvest. The total world loss of stored cereals, for which rats are largely responsible, is estimated at 33 million tons a year. But, given the circumstances, it may be as hard to save a bushel of wheat from the pests as to grow another bushel.

"The way to solve the problem is with food from the sea." In 1964 the harvest of fish was 56 million tons, compared with a grain harvest of about 1,000 million tons. An American Assembly publication[2] reports that this harvest could be quadrupled without de-

[2] Edmund A. Gullion, *Uses of the Seas,* The American Assembly (Englewood Cliffs, N.J.: Prentice-Hall, Inc., 1968), p. 56.

pleting fish stocks, given appropriate international conservation measures. The annual take of fish is increasing at a compounded rate of 6 per cent. The Bureau of Commercial Fisheries has developed fish protein concentrate (FPC), a highly nutritious food that is almost tasteless and odorless. The cost is low, approximately 25 cents per pound. Aquaculture, "farming the sea," is a growing science. Undoubtedly the use of food from the sea will continue to grow. But much time would be required before major reliance could be placed on the ocean as a means of meeting world food needs.

"The chemists will solve the problem with synthetic food." In time, perhaps. But for some years to come man will continue to get the great bulk of his food from conventional sources.

During recent years, agricultural production in the less-developed countries has been increasing at an overall rate of about 2.5 per cent per year. This is approximately the rate of population growth; the 2.5 per cent rate does not permit the less-developed nations to make any significant contribution to improved diets from their own production. But this annual rate of increased food production is large by comparison with any known previous period.

The President's Science Advisory Committee stated that a 4 per cent annual rate of growth in food production would be required to bring average diets up to presently established minimum levels of nutritional adequacy by 1980. An increase from 2.5 per cent to 4 per cent may seem like a relatively easy task. But this amounts to a 60 per cent increase in the rate of growth. The President's Science Advisory Committee says that to achieve a 4 per cent annual rate of increased food production in the less-developed countries, capital investments in these countries will have to increase from the current level of approximately 15 per cent to 19 per cent of the Gross National Product.

Although it is not likely that all the less-developed countries could achieve an annual rate of growth in production of 4 per cent, some of them are capable of doing so. A recent study of 26 developing nations, made by the Department of Agriculture, showed that between 1948 and 1963, 12 of the 26 developing nations had average annual rates of increase in excess of 4 per cent. These rates surpassed those achieved by now economically advanced nations during comparable periods of time. The 12 countries were Sudan, Mexico, Costa Rica, the Philippines, Tanganyika, Yugoslavia, Taiwan, Turkey, Venezuela, Thailand, Brazil, and Israel.

Projections of food production in the less-developed nations to the year 2000 are rather rare; the major ones have already been quoted. However, there are some projections to less distant dates, including a recent one that reflects somewhat more optimism than those released earlier. Martin Abel and Anthony S. Rojko of the U.S. Department of Agriculture made estimates of food production and consumption in the less-developed countries to the year 1980, specifying certain assumptions. They assume a population of about six billion people by the year 2000. They first project "historical" rates of increase in food production; then they step up the rate of improvement. The "moderate" rates of increase projected by Abel and Rojko assume that the less-developed countries "will place greater emphasis on agricultural development in the future, but do not imply a 'crash' program." The "rapid" improvement in production assumes a "greatly accelerated program of agricultural development."

Abel and Rojko translate their alternative projections into grain production, consumption and trade. They show that with "rapid" improvement, India could virtually free herself from reliance on imported grain by the year 1980. Based on "rapid" improvement they project a world grain surplus of 62.8 million metric tons by 1980. But recall our earlier point that in a long-run sense surplus is a fiction and that food and population come into balance.

This work serves to demonstrate how divergent are the projected results, depending on a small difference in the assumed rate of change. One begins to feel that he is involved in some kind of numbers game. As has been said, the adjusters in the food supply will undoubtedly wipe out all these discrepancies. The mathematics of projection carries with it the appearance of precision which, when dealing with such gross variables as food and people, can be quite deceptive.

But back to Abel and Rojko. The chief findings of their study are these:

If the historical rates of increase in grain production were to continue to 1980, the less-developed countries would require between 54 and 58 million metric tons of grain imports, an enormous amount. If the rate of increase in grain production were moderately improved, the less-developed countries would still require 52 million tons of grain imports by 1980. If the rate of growth in grain production gradually accelerated to 4 per cent annually by 1975 and continued at that rate to 1980, the less-developed countries would require about the same import levels as in 1964–65.

Some improvement in diets would be possible under each of these rates of increase in food production in the less-developed countries, with the grain imports that are projected. However, only when the increase in grain production accelerates to 4 per cent per year by 1975 and continues at that rate will the less-developed countries meet minimum calorie standards by 1980.

The size of the agricultural development task in the less-developed countries is tremendous. A near doubling of the historic rates of growth in food production would be required if these nations are to break their dependence on food aid, reach minimal levels of food consumption by 1980, and achieve higher rates of economic growth. This would require unprecedented rates of change in resource commitments. It would require massive efforts by many developing countries and considerable assistance from developed countries. The resources that would be required are far in excess of present levels of investment in agricultural development.

Improvement in rates of growth in food production in the less-developed countries will depend on the will and ability of these nations to take needed steps. It will require extremely large increases in:

1. The availability and use of a wide variety of such production in-

puts as improved seed, fertilizer, water, pesticides, machinery, and, where possible, land;

2. Public and private investment in research to create the technology and the trained teaching and extension personnel required to get the needed gains in agricultural productivity;

3. Investments to create the marketing, storage, and transportation systems required to support the desired agricultural production revolution and to provide the incentives to bring it about; and

4. Participation by the private trade in agribusiness ventures, both by domestic and foreign firms.

There is a special problem in the divergent agricultural circumstances as between the developed and the less-developed nations, that makes the Abel-Rojko 4 per cent rate of increase even harder to obtain. The developed nations are well along in the process of industrialization, and the agricultural revolution has been thereby facilitated. Industrial jobs were available. Rural people took these jobs, reduced the rural population and permitted those who continued farming to operate larger, more efficient farms. This trend will undoubtedly continue. But the less-developed countries are not industrialized, jobs are not available, and the growing population will pile up on farms already too small. In 1960 a farm population of 115 million in the developed countries had 37 million hectares of arable land, making 3.22 hectares per person. In the less-developed nations, 920 million farm people had 680 million hectares, or 0.74 per person. If one assumes that the total area farmed will not change substantially and if we accept the farm-nonfarm projections provided by Dr. Kristensen, then, by the year 2000 there will be 7.40 hectares per person in the developed countries and 0.46 in the less-developed countries. In other words, the average farmer in the developed countries now has about four times as much land as the farmer in the less-developed countries. By the year 2000 he will have 15 times as much. This is a situation that is explosive politically, as well as troublesome economically.

The people of the less-developed countries want to catch up with their more fortunate friends. But all the evidence is that the gap continues to widen. Everything seems to contribute to this result.

For example, consider recent government agricultural research budgets:[3]

	Government research budgets, cost per farmer
Taiwan	$ .49
India	.05
Japan	.69
Philippines	.27
Thailand	.05
Mexico	.35
United States	45.90

How can the gap be narrowed unless the countries that are now behind make a bigger effort to catch up?

But, just when one is about to be overcome by pessimism, some encouraging piece of news comes along. On May 29, 1968, Secretary of Agriculture Orville L. Freeman spoke thus to the Chicago Council on Foreign Relations:

High-yielding varieties of wheat, developed by the Rockefeller Foundation in Mexico, are proving adaptable across Asia as far north as Turkey and as far south as India. They are being planted in North Africa;

High-yielding tropical rice developed at the International Rice Research Institute in the Philippines is another, more recent, addition to the new varieties;

We estimate that in Turkey, India, Pakistan and the Philippines this crop year close to 20 million acres was planted to these high-yielding grains. That is well over 5 per cent of the total grain area in these countries. Next year, it is confidentially predicted the new varieties will be used on 30 to 40 million acres.

The impact of these new grains—which double, triple, and even quadruple yield—goes beyond crop yields. They alter basic farm prac-

[3] George Mehren, "One Dollar for Research," *International Agricultural Development*, No. 35 (Washington, D.C.: U.S. Department of Agriculture Cooperating with the Agency for International Development, September 1967), p. 3.

tices; they increase demand for fertilizer, pesticides, tillage machinery, pumps, engines, wells, and for such things as transistor radios and motorbikes, by farmers able for the first time to buy them with profits from increased production. They can become powerful engines of change in national economies in the less-developed countries.

Who knows? We may be on the threshold of changes—changes for the better—that are beyond our capacity to envision. Perhaps it is best to conclude the section on this note of hope. For hope is the one indispensible element in agricultural development.

The Problems of Food Distribution

All projections thus far reviewed reveal the disparate rate of agricultural progress in the developed as compared with the less-developed countries. This is most vividly portrayed by the reversal in the direction of net trade in grain between these two parts of the world, historical and projected, from sources already quoted:

Date	Direction of movement	Net movement of grain between the developed and the less-developed countries
		(million metric tons)
1934–38	From less-developed to developed countries	11 (actual)
1948–52	From developed to less-developed countries	4 (actual)
1957–58 to 1960–61	From developed to less-developed countries	15 (actual)
1980	From developed to less-developed countries	35 (projected by USDA)
2000	From developed to less-developed countries	68 (projected by USDA)

With the developed countries facing the prospect of continuing *over*-capacity and the less-developed countries facing the likelihood of *insufficiency,* the case for large-scale international trade, either commercial or on a concessionary basis, becomes very convincing. The possibilities of these two types of transfer will next be examined.

COMMERCIAL TRADE

The volume of commercial agricultural imports into a country has as its decisive element not some objective measure of need, but the desire for these products accompanied by the foreign exchange with which to purchase them, all within a public policy environment favorable to such trade.

The overwhelming quantities of commercial agricultural exports from the United States have long gone to other developed countries rather than to the less-developed food-deficit countries. They have gone where there were dollars to buy them. Only about one-third of our exports went to the less-developed countries. Most of this was Food for Peace.

Regarding the commercial international movement of agricultural products, the decisive question relates to comparative advantage. The United States, with its large farms, skilled farm operators, good equipment, good supporting institutions, fertile soil and favorable climate, clearly has an *absolute* advantage over India in the production of wheat. But, considering all costs and all other alternatives in the two countries, does the United States have a *comparative* advantage? The answer to questions like this in past years has generally been "no." It was believed that the developed countries, being industrialized, obviously had comparative advantage in industry. The less-developed countries, being overwhelmingly agricultural, were presumed to have comparative advantage in agriculture. Hence, it was thought, the net trade between these two great blocs of nations would consist of industrial products moving from the developed to the underdeveloped countries, with agricultural products moving in the opposite direction. Indeed, actual experience long confirmed this assessment. This was in fact the classic model for economic development, ever since the Industrial

Revolution. Some nations were to be industrialized; others were to be agricultural, "hewers of wood and drawers of water."

But in recent years, doubts have been cast on this view. The agricultural revolution, having had far greater relative impact on the already developed countries, has greatly altered the situation. Dr. Thorkil Kristensen says "It should also be recalled that, as mentioned above, by the year 2000 the developed countries as a group will have about three times as much agricultural land per head of population as the less-developed countries and they will also at that time be more richly endowed with capital and knowledge. They should, therefore, have a *comparative advantage* concerning agriculture, despite the large number of farm-workers per hectare in the poor countries. This being so, it would not be surprising if they were net exporters of food." [4] This view lends some support to the projections previously cited, which envision large exports from the developed to the less-developed world.

The ability of the less-developed nations to import food on a commercial basis will obviously depend on their ability to earn foreign exchange. This they must have the opportunity to do. They can earn foreign exchange with industrial products, if markets are available. With abundant supplies of low-cost labor, with plentiful raw materials, with modern managerial skills and with capital increasingly available, they may have considerable comparative advantage in certain types of industrial products. They clearly have comparative advantage in a number of agricultural products that cannot be produced in the developed countries, or cannot be produced efficiently or in sufficient volume to meet needs. In this connection, there is a popular illusion to the effect that United States foreign trade in agricultural products consists overwhelmingly of exports and that these exports constitute an enormous share of our farm output. This is not true; the United States imports vast quantities of farm products. In 1967, for example, the figures were reported as follows in various publications of the Department of Agriculture:

[4] Kristensen, *International Journal of Agrarian Affairs*, p. 140.

	Billion dollars
Total value of U.S. farm production	42.5
Total value of U.S. agricultural exports, commercial and non-commercial	6.4
Total value of agricultural products imported into the U.S.	4.5
Net agricultural exports	1.9
Net agricultural exports as a percentage of U.S. farm production	4.5

Approximately half of all agricultural products imported into the United States are commodities not produced domestically, for example, coffee, tea and cocoa. The other half of United States agricultural imports compete directly with our own production: sugar, beef, wool, vegetables, canned ham and pork, livestock, tobacco, and vegetable oils. The three countries supplying the highest value of imports are all less-developed countries—Brazil, Mexico and the Philippines. The fourth and fifth largest suppliers are Canada and Australia. Then follow Colombia and New Zealand. Clearly, agricultural markets in the United States are a major source of foreign exchange for a number of the less-developed countries.

All of this makes a powerful case for:

1. Balanced economic growth in the less-developed countries, which couples industrialization with agricultural improvement, and
2. Liberal trade policies that permit the development of those agricultural enterprises and those industries which are most likely to be viable.

But even when all the favorable possibilities are postulated, it does not seem likely that the less-developed countries will find it possible to generate sufficient foreign exchange, over and above imperative needs for capital goods, to buy the enormous amounts of food that have been projected as necessary.

Some people think that American commercial agricultural exports to the less-developed countries could be increased if, like

Avis, we would try harder. It would be difficult to see how we could try much harder than we have during the last decade. Trade missions, trade fairs, promotional efforts and market studies have been tried. The difficulty is a lack of buying power.

FOOD AID

The analysis seems to be taking us down an inexorable line of thought: The need for food imports in the less-developed countries will be very great, the developed countries are faced with excess capacity, and the commercial markets seem incapable of moving the necessary volume. Therefore, the inference is, let us supply the food free of charge, or for foreign currency.

In support of this view are a large number of citizens with various motives:

Warm-hearted people, moved by compassion for the less fortunate;
Farmers, who see the possibility of an overseas "market" for their production;
Agribusiness firms, who would gain by serving an agriculture operating at maximum production;
Amateur diplomats, who think the United States would gain international good will by a large-scale food-aid program.

Thus there has developed a vision or a myth, depending on how it is viewed. American farmers would be freed of limitations on output, to their immense gratification. Such food as was not needed domestically would be bought from the farmers at a good price, loaded on ships, wrapped in the American Flag, and sent to Calcutta. There the people would be, waiting on the dock to receive it, grateful to us for supplying it, and, out of gratitude, voting with us in the United Nations.

This is a mighty myth, needing careful examination. To examine this myth we must first describe the Food for Peace program.

Advantages of Direct Food Aid—Direct food aid, popularly named Food for Peace, was formalized in 1954 in Public Law 480. A brief record of that operation is appropriate (Table 8).

TABLE 8. *Exports Under the Food for Peace Program, 1955–1966.*

Exports of agricultural products from the U.S.

	In billions of dollars			In percentages		
	Food for Peace	Other	Total	Food for Peace	Other	Total
1955	.8	2.3	3.1	26	74	100
1956	1.3	2.2	3.5	38	62	100
1957	1.9	2.8	4.7	41	59	100
1958	1.2	2.8	4.0	30	70	100
1959	1.2	2.5	3.7	33	67	100
1960	1.3	3.2	4.5	28	72	100
1961	1.5	3.4	4.9	30	70	100
1962	1.5	3.6	5.1	30	70	100
1963	1.5	3.6	5.1	29	71	100
1964	1.5	4.6	6.1	25	75	100
1965	1.7	4.4	6.1	28	72	100
1966	1.6	5.1	6.7	24	76	100
1955–1966*	17.2	40.4	57.6	30	70	100

* Totals may not check, due to rounding.

Source: *Twelve Years of Achievement Under Public Law 480*, ERS-Foreign 202, Economic Research Service, U.S. Department of Agriculture, Washington, D.C.; November 1967.

The program has leveled off at a little more than a billion and a half dollars a year, an amount approximately equal to the annual value of farm products grown in the State of Nebraska. On the average, about three shiploads of Public Law 480 food move out of American ports each day, bound for any of a large number of less-developed countries. The commodities go to millions of people in more than 100 countries. The aid constitutes no more than a small part of the food supply in any receiving country. In 1966 the major commodities were:[5]

[5] *Twelve Years of Achievement Under Public Law 480.*

	Million dollars' worth
Wheat and wheat flour	937.1
Oilseeds and products	136.6
Cotton	123.6
Feed grains, including products	113.6
Dairy products	93.5
Tobacco	89.9
Other	121.6
Total	1,615.9

Obviously the program is not limited to food, as is attested by the presence of cotton and tobacco in this list. Most of these commodities are sold for foreign currency, some of which is used in support of United States programs in these countries and a part of which accumulates in our hands, unspent. Some of the commodities are donated by the United States government to other governments, for disaster relief. Some are donated directly to needy individuals through charitable organizations like CARE and the National Catholic Welfare Conference. Some are sold for long-term low-interest credit. Some are bartered for "strategic and critical materials" that go into our stockpile, in some cases far in excess of any conceivable need. Of this operation it has been said that we barter food, which we can't use, for non-food items, which we can't use.

What has been accomplished by this program?

Authentic needs have been met and lives have been saved. For example, the monsoon failed on the Indian subcontinent for two years running, 1965 and 1966. The United States responded by shipping the equivalent of one-fifth of its wheat harvest, feeding 60 million Indians for nearly two years. This record shipment, the largest ever between two countries, was sufficient to stave off famine.

Some diplomatic gains were achieved. Favorable settlement of an international political problem in Trieste was accomplished, for example, with the help of food aid. There have been instances when American food helped quiet outbreaks of disorder abroad and permitted a responsible political party to stay in power.

Foreign currencies generated by the programs have been used in support of American overseas programs. The Department of Agriculture puts this figure at $222 million for the year 1967. This reduces the size of the American outlay of dollars abroad. The programs have thus been beneficial rather than harmful in their effect on the balance of payments. Aid-in-kind, of which food aid is our leading example, involves a cost in resources (which are abundant) but not a cost in foreign exchange (which is scarce).

Some economic development has been induced. As a condition of receiving the aid, recipient countries have been required to expand their own agricultural programs—research, education, resource development and the like. Some of the currencies have been loaned to American business firms and invested in the less-developed countries, with beneficial effects for all parties.

Storage costs on American surpluses have been cut by the program, and the size of the government acreage limitation program has been reduced.

These are sizeable accomplishments, and a record of which the United States can well be proud. But the program has leveled off at a little more than a billion and a half dollars a year. It peaked in 1957, more than a decade ago. If the case for direct food aid is so persuasive and if the experience with it has produced the above-mentioned benefits, why has the program not grown?

Disadvantages of Direct Food Aid—direct food aid is an economic invention of considerable importance. Like other inventions, it has disadvantages as well as advantages. These disadvantages, which explain the fact that the program has reached a plateau rather than having continued to grow, will now be reviewed. The disadvantages, perhaps less visible than the advantages, appear in both the supplying and the receiving country.

One obvious disadvantage to the donor countries is cost. The program runs over a billion and a half dollars a year. But here it is important to realize that, given the inclination of the American government to provide income assurances to our farmers and given our excess productive capacity, the cost of the Food for Peace program is not a net cost. We handle our excess agricultural capacity

in part by our crop reduction programs and in part by the Food for
Peace program. If we were to curtail the Food for Peace program
in an effort to save money, and were not willing to see farm incomes
reduced, we would have to increase our crop reduction program,
at considerable additional cost. What is the nature of this trade-off?
According to a study at Purdue University, done by Richard Ed-
wards, the cost of preventing the production of a bushel of corn is
about $1.03. In May of 1968 the farm price of corn in the United
States was $1.09 per bushel. By reason of the various kinds of slip-
page in the crop control program, it costs almost as much to prevent
the production of a bushel of grain as it does to grow it. Of course,
transportation to port, processing, packaging, and ocean freight add
to the cost. Cost is a disadvantage to the donor country, but, all
things considered, not so great a cost as may first appear.

Another disadvantage to donor countries is the fact that food aid
programs serve to rationalize unsound farm policies. The commodities to be exported are accumulated not on the basis of the
need for them abroad or the foreign policy interests of the United
States, but on the basis of which commodity has the greatest political power or the greatest surplus-generating power, which is
approximately the same thing. The result can be a food aid program not well suited either to donor or recipient. And since the
Food for Peace program empties the bin, surplus-building farm
programs can be continued in existence. Recently, Food for Peace
has become more of a foreign aid program and less a surplus-disposal
program.

Another disadvantage to donor countries is that they may be giving away, in part, what they would otherwise sell. Recipient countries contract to take "usual marketings" in the form of commercial
imports, based on some historical experience, as a condition for receiving aid. These "usual marketings" tend to become fixed over
time. Normally there would be some commercial growth in the
market, with dollar earnings for the donor country or for other commercial exporters. But with the "usual marketings" provision, the
growth in volume tends to be in the form of donations.

Perhaps the greatest disadvantage of the program is that if it becomes excessively large, a bond of dependency is built between donor and recipient, a bond that neither can afford to break. The donor cannot easily terminate the program because a considerable number of its citizens have become economically dependent thereon. And if the recipient country has come to rely heavily on the assistance, termination would mean starvation for many, with all the human misery and all the adverse diplomatic consequences attendant thereto. In the eyes of the world, the donor would stand accused of crass indifference. Thus the program might have to be continued, even though both parties might wish it were not in existence.

There is, in the Orient, a tradition to the effect that when you have saved a person's life you become responsible for him thereafter. There may be some of this in direct food aid.

The foregoing disadvantages to the donor countries probably will be convincing to the average reader, if he is from a donor country. But, he will think, how can there be disadvantages to the recipient country? A country with a large and growing population, with a poorly developed agriculture, with widespread hunger and malnutrition, with food riots active or incipient, with a depleted supply of foreign exchange—would it not want all the free food it could get?

The answer is "no." And the reason is sound. If a less-developed country takes a large amount of free food, prices of farm products in that country will be depressed. Farmers will be discouraged from undertaking improved crop practices. Food production will not increase as it should. Dependence on donated food will grow. The recipient country may in time become so dependent on the donor nation that it loses its autonomy. If India becomes critically dependent upon the United States for its food supply, will she feel free to chart her own course, diplomatically? Where would she be if her benefactor, upon whom she has become dependent, should suddenly decide to terminate the food aid program?

The less-developed countries have asked themselves these searching questions. And, in general, they have made the tough—and correct—decision to accept some degree of want and hunger rather than inhibit their own agricultural production and lose their autonomy in international councils. Many of them have just thrown off colonial status; they are not about to accept what may look to them like imperialism in a new form. And for this they deserve much credit. Their experience with hunger is greater than ours, and should not be lightly dismissed. Prudence is needed in this business, as well as compassion. Many warm-hearted Americans would overwhelm the less-developed countries with our generosity. But a warm heart is not enough; a level head is also needed.

If this seems incomprehensible, it may help to invert the problem. Suppose the United States were a food deficit country. Would the Secretary of Agriculture welcome great volumes of free food from abroad, to depress our prices and inhibit our agricultural development? He certainly would not. Nor should we expect the Minister of Food in some less-developed country to do so.

Strange as it seems, it is at least as hard to give food away constructively as it is to sell it.

Some direct food aid the recipient nations want. How much? As much as they need to meet some natural disaster. As much as they can absorb without seriously impairing their own agricultural development. As much as they can take without becoming dependent on their benefactor. An amount of such limited size that the termination thereof would not mean, for them, unacceptable hardship. Most recipient countries have stayed within these boundaries. A few, in desperate circumstances, have overstepped these bounds and are now in all probability permanent relief clients of the United States.

A QUESTION OF VOLUME

This brings us to the most important statement in the present section of this chapter. *The major limitation on the size of direct food aid is the difficulty of using this food constructively in the recipient nation.* It is growing realization of this fact that has made food aid more of a conscious part of our foreign aid program and less an adjunct of domestic farm policy.

The long-run effect of food aid on the well-being of a recipient country is in the form of a curve, as shown in Figure 1.

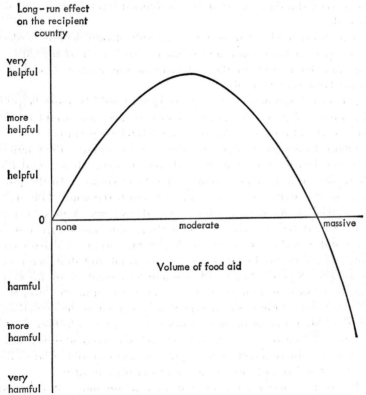

FIGURE 1. Schematic Representation of the Relationship between the Volume of Food Aid and the Long-Run Consequences for the Recipient Country.

If a relationship is linear, one need not reckon where he is on the scale; the nth increment will give the same result as the first. With linear relationships, if something is good, more is better, and the most one could supply would yield the greatest possible good. But most public programs are not so. Direct food aid is not so. Judgment is needed as to where one is on the scale, and whether the activity should be held at the established level, increased or decreased.

The direct food aid program, as a result of considerable wisdom on the part of both donor and recipient, has been held at relatively moderate levels and, in the judgment of this analyst, has on the whole been very helpful.

It does not follow that a larger program would be more helpful. Nor does it follow that because a massive program would be disastrous, therefore the entire program should be terminated.

Figure 1 purports to show, for the *recipient* country, the relationship between food aid volume and consequences. How would this chart look from the standpoint of the *donor* country? In the judgment of this writer, it would look very much the same. The maximum good comes from a moderate-sized program. A massive program would be very costly, would throw our agriculture out of joint and would create a class of dependent nations. A sharply curtailed program would forego economic, social and diplomatic opportunities. So both donor and recipient have good reason for keeping the volume at a moderate level, somewhere near the level that has prevailed. This is the reason that the program has remained, since its inception, at a level between $1.5 and $2.0 billion, under two political parties, three presidents, and numerous administrators. This is in spite of a continual tug of war between some who would vastly expand it and some who would sharply curtail it.

Recipient countries reason that they retain more of their autonomy if food aid is provided multilaterally, as through the Food and Agriculture Organization of the United Nations. This is true, and consequently considerable support exists for a large-scale FAO food-aid program. Responsibility for food aid does not lie solely with the United States. Other developed nations have engaged in some food aid, though not nearly so much as the United States. The case for food aid provided by a number of nations is a convincing one. But it does not necessarily follow that the several supplying nations should undertake a large food-aid program in a formal multilateral fashion. Such a program would not relieve the recipient country of the adverse effect of excessive volume. And multilateral programs, with decisions as to commodities and recipients made by an international council rather than by national officials, arouse little enthusiasm on the part of national legislators.

SELF-HELP WITH ASSISTANCE

Our analysis thus carries us to this conclusion: that while direct food aid can be very helpful if wisely administered and kept at a moderate level, it is not a solution to the world food problem. The massive transfers envisioned by each of the three projections seem unlikely to develop. If the food problem is to be met, it must be solved, with our help, primarily in the hungry nations themselves.

This seems a possible thing. It may be that now, when the world is most alarmed about hunger, that ancient enemy is already in retreat. And the two events may be related. The alarm may have summoned the needed resources. The historian may write that ours was the generation that moved mankind out from under the Malthusian shadow. Certainly our generation is the first to see that this is possible.

J. George Harrar and Sterling Wortman

3

Expanding Food Production in Hungry Nations: The Promise, the Problems

Opportunities for Expansion

There is no doubt that less-developed countries now can, if they so choose, obtain dramatic increases in levels of food produc-

J. GEORGE HARRAR, *President of The Rockefeller Foundation since 1960, has been associated with that organization since 1943. In that year he was appointed the first director of the Foundation's agricultural program in Mexico, and ten years later he was made head of the Foundation's entire international program in agriculture. Before joining the Foundation, Dr. Harrar taught botany and plant pathology at the University of Puerto Rico, the University of Minnesota, Virginia Polytechnic Institute, and Washington State University. The recipient of numerous honors and awards from foreign governments in recognition of his contributions to world agriculture, he is also the author of* Strategy for the Conquest of Hunger *(1967) and (with E. C. Stakman)* Principles of Plant Pathology *(1957).*

STERLING WORTMAN *is Director for Agricultural Sciences of The Rockefeller Foundation. A specialist in plant genetics, Dr. Wortman has headed corn improvement work in the Foundation's Mexican Agricultural Program, has served as Associate Director of the International Rice Research*

tion and thereby stimulate economic development as they relieve
the misery of their people. A vast reservoir of scientific agricultural
information and capability is available which can be quickly brought
into action, if adapted by each country to its own local conditions.

The food problem is most urgent, of course, in those nations or
regions where population density is high and the land/man ratio
most unfavorable. Here, the only reasonable alternative to still
greater human distress is a rapid increase in yields per unit area
through use of all the beneficial force of modern science.

Some of these nations are beginning to realize that it is now
possible to move rather suddenly from subsistence farming, with
its low and static yields, to a dynamic, market-oriented, highly productive agriculture—one offering a sound base for general economic
development and hence leading to creation of the wealth needed
to pay for essential public health, educational, and other social
services.

The time is now right for mounting large and vigorous campaigns
to increase average yields of food grains in most of the developing
countries. The progress already made—in Southeast Asia with improved rice varieties, in India and Pakistan with wheat, rice, corn,
and sorghum, in Latin America with corn, wheat, and potatoes, and
in East Africa with corn, wheat, and sorghum—provides ample
evidence of what can be done. These accomplishments are visible
and measurable; their impact can be assessed in economic and social
terms.

EXPLOITING AVAILABLE TECHNOLOGY

The basic materials and the technology required to mount crop
and animal production campaigns wherever needed are at hand.
Although these materials usually must be adapted or modified by
scientists to meet local requirements, the techniques for making the
modifications are better known today than ever before.

Much of the world's diverse germplasm, or basic material, of the

*Institute, and Director of the Pineapple Research Institute of Hawaii. He
is a member of the Agricultural Board of the National Academy of Sciences and is Vice President of the Agribusiness Council, Inc.*

major crop species has been collected, partially evaluated, and stored in central vaults. These "germplasm banks" constitute a primary resource of enormous potential value. Thanks to the science of genetics, plant-breeding techniques are now so well developed that capable scientists can use available germplasm of virtually every important food plant to create new, improved types, tailored to meet the unique requirements of each season of each region in each nation. Admittedly, the task is formidable; but it can be done just as surely as engineers can build a superhighway across a nation or space scientists can place a satellite in orbit.

In achieving control of some plant diseases and pests, man has acquired sufficient knowledge and enough technical and organizational skill to know that the damage now inflicted by many others, which annually cause tremendous losses, can be minimized by developing resistant types of plants or by devising appropriate means of chemical control. And, out of chemistry has come a vast and ever-increasing array of compounds that, if wisely used, will permit control of many major plant diseases, insect pests, and weeds without undue danger to man or harm to his environment. With entomologists and plant pathologists becoming ever more knowledgeable about the basic characteristics and behavior of many of the principal organisms that attack man's food sources, rapid progress should be possible in devising ways to combat countless other plant diseases and pests that so far remain as neglected problems.

Animal pathologists and parasitologists likewise have deepened and broadened their knowledge, and applied it to benefit the health and increase the comfort of domestic animals. Useful antibiotics having high specificity are being identified, and knowledge about the usefulness of antibiotics generally has been greatly amplified.

With advances in physics, geology, chemistry, and biology, a sizable amount of information has been acquired on the nature of soils as they affect plant and animal productivity. Many of the roles of specific nutrients are known, and techniques for correcting deficiencies or excesses have been devised. At the same time, advances in the technology of chemical fertilizer production have resulted in substantially lower unit costs. World production of the three major nutrients—nitrogen, phosphoric acid, and potash—has risen sharply since World War II, from 7.5 million tons in 1945–46 to about 40 million tons in 1965–66; as of 1966, however, capacity for production still exceeded effective demand.

The relatively recent development of power-driven machinery permits farmers to dominate ever greater land areas, to shorten the time required for land preparation, cultivation, and harvest, and to clear land or plow to depths previously impossible or impracticable with the lower power output of animals, or of man himself.

Improvements in pump design and extension of power grids contribute to the ease of supply of needed potable and irrigation water either from surface or subsurface sources. Man increasingly is learning to harness the great and lesser rivers to effect flood control, to provide irrigation water, and to supply needed electrical power. Knowledge of the management of soils and water to remedy or prevent problems of salinity is also improving.

Thus, the technical resources for mounting food production campaigns, wherever needed, are amply available.

MODERNIZATION OF AGRICULTURE

Modern agriculture has become a complex, highly sophisticated industry, and must be treated as such. Each component—technical or economic—is vital to the total process, and the significant lack of any one of them can disrupt the entire system. Efficient agriculture requires the maintenance of a biological and physical equilibrium in the production system, even when changes occur in technology, the terms of farm trade, or the availability of inputs. This does not come about by any easy combinations of seeds, manpower, soil, water, sunlight, and air. Each component must be provided at opportune times, in the appropriate amounts, by correct methods, at reasonable cost, and with good judgment in operations. Too often, the sophisticated task of combining these components into highly productive systems has been left to relatively unschooled farmers or to inadequately trained extension men. Clearly, however, it is a complex endeavor that must receive the attention of agricultural scientists, economists, and administrators.

Moreover, these systems cannot function as planned unless other, equally important factors are provided; these include price incentives, credit, transport, markets, needed industrial products, and improved educational opportunities.

Unfortunately, the biological and other phases of modern agriculture are not well enough understood, even by many agriculturists and administrators who direct agricultural improvement programs and by legislators who vote financial appropriations for them.

Food is produced, not in air-conditioned factories, but in open fields where plants and animals, being living things and not mere physical and chemical substances, are subject to the vagaries of weather and are menaced always by a wide variety of other living things—bacteria, fungi, insects, and the semi-living viruses, and by birds, rodents, and other higher animals. Furthermore, there are scores of crop plants, each with numerous varieties, and each has its own combinations of environmental requirements. Of the basic food crops—such as wheat, rice, maize, sorghums, millets, potatoes, beans and other legumes, cassava, plantains, sugarcane and sugarbeets—each kind has its particular requirements of soil and water and nutrients, of temperature and light and length of growing season, and of protective measures against weeds and pests and plant diseases. In many respects it is easier to run a factory than it is to run a farm, for men can dominate a factory but man has not established complete dominion over nature.

There are those, of course, who put their faith in non-conventional agriculture, in the biological or chemical synthesis of foods. Undeniably, progress is being made toward farming the oceans for new sources of protein to be found in fish, shellfish, and unicellular algae, toward synthesizing proteins from petroleum with microorganisms, and toward developing leaf protein as a supplemental food—to mention only some examples of the research currently under way. The time has not yet come, however, when factories can produce the bulk of basic foods that more than three billion human beings require. We cannot wait for potential miracles while millions of people hunger. For many decades still we must depend on conventional agriculture and its improvement.

FROM STUDY TO ACTION

In the past, there has been an unfortunate tendency to study food crisis situations exhaustively and to keep postponing efforts to apply available knowledge in national programs promising definitive results within a reasonable period of time. Today, little is to be gained from further in-depth studies and surveys. Enough is now known to assure the success of properly conceived production programs, adapted to local needs and backed up by training of manpower and by solution through research of new problems as they are identified.

Essentials for National Production Programs

Acceleration of agricultural production must be the primary responsibility of individual nations, for only they can set the necessary new policies and only through national institutions can the farmers be reached, personnel be trained in adequate numbers, and technical problems unique to the country be handled.

NATIONAL COMMITMENT

The primary requirement in converting an underproductive agricultural system to one which takes full advantage of all of the available technologies and other essential elements is a clear-cut national commitment. Farmers, extension agents, scientists, and educators cannot bring about the establishment of a sound agricultural industry without the enthusiastic support of the national leadership. Working together, it is possible for them to evaluate present situations, establish future goals, set priorities, and undertake direct action for designated purposes. Well-conceived plans must be supported with adequate funds to enable the technical leadership and the other associates in the total scheme to function efficiently and promptly. When national authorities provide the essential elements available locally, then it becomes possible for technical assistance agencies, public or private, bilateral or multilateral, to cooperate effectively in the adaptation of existing knowledge, technologies, and biological materials in the implementation of a demonstrably progressive and effective program.

It has been repeatedly shown that political, business, professional, and scientific leaders within the several less-developed countries are keenly aware of their needs and their problems and that many are desirous of bringing about change which will improve the national social and economic condition. Unfortunately, they are under heavy pressure to make progress on all fronts in an attempt to satisfy national expectations. Almost inevitably, resources are inadequate for total requirements so that there is an imbalance between demand and supply. All too often the agricultural sector is neglected since it tends to be remote, unorganized, disadvantaged, and without a strong voice in the national scene. Public works, education, public health, and military requirements usually occupy positions of priority in respect to the demand on the public purse. Important as these may be, in the long run they can be only partially successful if the predominantly agrarian nations do not fully support their agricultural industry which is so fundamental to their economic well-being. Indeed, stability of government itself may well depend upon the degree of attention paid to the agricultural industry and its workers.

Once an integrated approach to the problems of full agricultural production has been established, it can be predicted that total production will rise each year with commensurate benefits to the national economy. If at the same time progress can be made in stabilizing populations and lowering birth rates, then the benefits of agricultural development will be dramatically enhanced.

CONTINUOUS ADAPTIVE RESEARCH

By "adaptive research" we mean that research which seeks effective solutions to urgent and pressing problems—as distinguished from pure research, whose objective is knowledge for its own sake. In the case of agriculture, adaptive research includes: the development of food crop varieties that have the greatest productive capacity under local conditions and are resistant to the major pests and pathogens which commonly threaten the productivity of local varieties; the identification, through studies of soils, soil and water management, and performance of crop varieties, of practices that will maximize yields in each season of each region; the determination, through studies of the physiology of plants, of nutritional requirements and how these can be satisfied; and studies of the quality of harvested products and means of improvement.

Adaptive research is essential in many cases in order to take full advantage of plant materials now available in germplasm banks or the equivalent. For example, varieties of wheat and rice developed for use in temperate climates may have the important characteristics of earliness, short stature, stiff straw, and high inherent yielding ability, but nevertheless may be unsuited to the tropics because they lack the ability to thrive where days are short. Under these circumstances, it becomes a function of adaptive research to add this characteristic by means of breeding methods. Or, the varieties may have all the characteristics needed for high productivity and yet not be of the quality that will gain them acceptance in new areas; again, adaptive research must be put to work to supply the missing ingredient. Many varieties of wheat and rice have thus been tailored to meet the requirements of regions far from those in which the varieties originated.

Unhappily, in many of the less-developed countries there has been no proper balance between adaptive and pure, or fundamental, research; usually, the latter has been emphasized almost to the exclusion of the former. Fundamental research is, of course, exceedingly important and must be conducted wherever feasible because it is the basis of all other forms of research and experimentation. The fact remains that the practical problems of agricultural production can be solved only through adaptive research; they cannot be solved where there is heavy and lopsided emphasis on fundamental research, particularly when this is carried out under the handicaps that exist in most of the less-developed countries.

In all too many instances, research scientists in agriculture have attempted to copy some of the less fortunate tendencies of their counterparts in the basic sciences, by learning more and more about less and less in fields, which although important to science, are relatively unimportant to the immediate economic requirements of their nations. In some countries, it is even considered provincial to emphasize adaptive research, especially when to do so would mean that, for a time at least, the limited resources available for all research would have to be devoted solely to adaptive research. Obviously, this point of view totally ignores the existing food crisis, which demands that the food-deficit nations make rapid changes if they are to develop their economic potential and begin to catch up in terms of production figures. If the newer nations fail to emphasize the kinds of research and its application which will lead directly to increased production, they will be doomed to an alms-seeking economy, forever dependent on foodstuffs obtained from abroad on a gift or loan basis. Such imports may provide a temporary solution but, in the long run, reliance on them may undermine the technological and economic structure of the receiving nation.

The effects of programs of adaptive agricultural research are immediately visible in terms of increased production. Farmers using the same amount of land are enabled, with modern methods, materials, and information, to increase their average yields by very substantial percentages, often by as much as 200 to 400 per cent. This increase benefits not only the farmer but also his community and his nation. If at the same time the farmer is also provided with facilities for the transport and marketing of his surplus, he is enabled to improve his own situation still further. As the process continues, the whole economy profits from the increased supplies of agricultural products in the form of foods, feeds, and fibers.

Once the basic need for adaptive research and its immediate application to the local requirements is understood and practiced, more attention can be given to fundamental research—which, of course, must also be continued in developed nations. The new knowledge gained from this basic research can then be fed into the adaptive hopper so that as it proves to be of value, it can at once be incorporated into the production pattern of the nation.

SOUND AGRICULTURAL EDUCATION

As developing nations attempt to move quickly toward modernization of their agriculture, their institutions of higher education—either existing or newly created—must assume leading roles. If they do not, progress will be stifled. Where an agrarian way of life predominates, opportunities for good agricultural education are essential in order that the national agriculture may be able to count on the services of well-qualified young men and women. Thus, it is imperative that each country's agricultural institutions be continually improved and, furthermore, that they be developed realistically in terms of the requirements of the nation.

In many of these nations, there is a unique and pressing problem related to agricultural education. Young persons entering the colleges of agriculture often come either from subsistence farms, where technical agriculture was essentially unknown, or from the cities; thus they have little or no skill in managing crops or animals for high productivity. At the colleges, they are taught by faculty members who share this background and who, even though they hold advanced degrees from major universities in developed nations, nevertheless have not been afforded opportunities to become skilled in the art and practice of technical agriculture. Consequently, present and past graduates are handicapped by lack of understanding of the problems facing the farm producer and are not equipped with the new information that should increase the productivity and profitability of farming. Because they are not themselves experienced in production techniques, they cannot show the farmer how to use new technology, nor can they diagnose problems and prescribe useful remedies. In too many nations the agricultural graduates, equipped with some knowledge but without skill in its application, are of as little value as would be medical doctors who had never served an internship.

The modern agricultural scientist needs a thorough training in the basic sciences that underpin agriculture, including mathematics, physics, chemistry, and biology in their elementary and more advanced forms. He also needs a general knowledge of other sciences and the humanities. As he progresses toward the higher levels of agricultural education, he must furthermore be able to integrate the various components of his education so that ultimately he can put what he knows to meaningful use and can communicate this knowledge to those seeking assistance. The older idea that an agricultural scientist was merely a practical practitioner of production has long since given way to the realization that an agricultural scientist must be qualified as a professional, just as professionals in other fields must be. He must be able to synthesize and analyze, to write and communicate, and to carry on research that ultimately may be used to improve agricultural efficiency and benefit the economy. Some agricultural scientists must devote their energies to research and investigation, seeking solutions to the problems that limit agricultural production. Others must adapt the findings of research, apply them to the local scene and demonstrate the needed improvements that are possible. Others must dedicate their energies, enthusiasm, and knowledge to teaching new generations of youth to be effective in improving national agricultural production. Finally, another group of well-trained agricultural specialists must function as extension agents.

The college of agriculture must assume leadership of several types. It must assemble the information, concepts, and skills emanating from all the sciences, applied and fundamental, which could contribute to the progress of the region served. It must test available technology and through research in its laboratories and on its experiment station develop new methods and materials so that course offerings will be relevant to local needs. The growing body of knowledge and of skills in its application must be preserved and effectively transmitted to the substantial numbers of young people who must become increasingly competent in the practice of professional agriculture.

The importance of another role, that of service to the region, cannot be overemphasized. Since the college of agriculture in developing countries must be equipped with a high proportion of the nation's scarce professional talent, it is essential that this resource be brought to bear on the most urgent and immediate problems blocking increases in agricultural productivity. The experiment station is the field laboratory where the solutions can be sought by the faculty and where students can, by participating in technical projects, gain the competence and confidence to practice their profession effectively. The experiment station, therefore, is as critical to a college of agriculture as is a teaching hospital to a medical college. One of the best measures of the quality of a college of agriculture is the caliber of its experiment station and staff; the caliber of the experiment station, in turn, must be measured by the relevance of its research to urgent needs and by its impact on agricultural development in the region.

Obviously, the value of research is not realized until the findings are applied. Therefore, it is important that the activities of the university or college experiment station be closely interlocked with those of the extension service and of experiment stations of the ministry of agriculture. In tropical regions, colleges of agriculture and their experiment stations face one difficulty not encountered in temperate climates: because the field research program is a year-round activity, there is no long winter period during which research scientists can teach and also prepare for the next summer's field work. Research professorships must therefore be provided to enable scientists to give full-time, twelve-month attention to critical research efforts. Such faculty members can play an important role in the educational process by supervising students' participation in research projects, at the graduate or undergraduate level, by taking part in seminars, and by giving occasional lectures or conducting advanced courses. If the research program is to be effective, however, these research leaders must be allowed to give their projects the continuing attention which is a prerequisite to success.

As highly productive new technology is developed and demonstrated on college or other experiment stations, a further critical responsibility becomes apparent: substantial numbers of past graduates must be given the opportunity to gain the technical experience previously unavailable to them. Some colleges in the tropics are now arranging for such persons to return to the experiment stations for periods of several months—sometimes detailed there by the agencies or companies employing them—so that they can participate intensively in the experimental program and acquire the new knowledge they so urgently need. Such programs are most effective if developed and supported cooperatively by the colleges and the employers.

Increasingly, the colleges of agriculture in the developing nations must become centers for postgraduate education leading to advanced degrees. Scientists and educators will be needed in ever larger numbers, and it is important that they be thoroughly familiar with local problems and that the research components of their studies contribute to local progress. Advanced courses offered at institutions in developed nations often have little relevance to needs in the students' homelands; furthermore, study abroad is expensive. Nevertheless, until local institutions are staffed, no other solution is available. It is therefore alarming that so few graduate students from developing countries are being trained in agriculture. For example, according to the National Institute of Education, less than 4 per cent of foreign students at U.S. universities in 1966 were in agriculture, as compared with 22 per cent in engineering, 20 per cent in the humanities, 18 per cent in the natural and physical sciences, 15 per cent in the social sciences, and 5 per cent in the medical sciences.

The land-grant colleges of the United States have a brilliant record of service through education, research, and extension tailored to the needs of their own states. As they evolved, they gained great respect, appreciation, and broad financial support; they are now under even heavier pressure to contribute their services to agriculture and to the rest of the nation's economy. Many of these U.S. colleges have been and should continue to be effective in assisting institutions in the developing countries to make their educational, research, and extension activities similarly responsive to the needs of their regions. But with any set of problems, the solution must be worked out in particular terms. The U.S. land-grant model as it exists today cannot be applied in template fashion to situations overseas; it can, however, be effectively adapted. And, the land-grant college principle of establishing leadership in economic development through coordinated education, research, and extension is valid everywhere.

EFFECTIVE EXTENSION

The increasingly available and productive new systems of agricultural technology can have tremendous impact, but only if there is an extension service forming the vital link between the research center and the farmers. The extension agent is therefore a critical element in a successful agricultural industry.

To convince well-educated farm entrepreneurs of the value of the new technology is, of course, comparatively simple. Not only are they readily reached by conventional extension techniques—technical bulletins, field days, newspapers and magazines, radio and television, agribusiness promotions—but also they are competent to discuss experiments in progress with the research scientists themselves.

The real problem is how to convince the great majority of poorly educated farmers, who have only a small landholding or a tenancy arrangement and seldom, if ever, travel any distance from home. With this group of farmers, the message of the new technology must be brought to them directly and made clear visually, not just in written terms. This means that, to be effective, the extension agent in a developing country must be sufficiently experienced to be able to demonstrate the new practices himself, without reliance on the research center. Let us suppose, for example, that the extension agent is responsible for explaining the new rice technology to farmers in an area of Southeast Asia; what kinds of competence must he have? Specifically, he must be able to show the farmers how to prepare a seedbed, how to treat seed, how to identify and obtain seed of recommended varieties, how to transplant in rows, how to control several different insect pests, and how to harvest, dry, store, and market the product. He must also be able to diagnose problems in the field and to recommend corrective measures. In other words, he must be a rice production specialist, functioning on the basis of in-depth experience that probably was acquired during at least several months of intensive training at an experiment station. He is thus much more than a "communications" specialist who, with the benefit of a short course on rice production, can be only minimally effective in the same circumstances.

It is essential that extension services in the developing nations be staffed with experienced, highly competent men who have ready access to the resources of experiment stations and, in some cases, even have a research station as their home base. Only in this way can a two-way flow of research results to farmers and of field problems to scientists be expedited.

Fortunately—and apparently to the surprise of some—many small farmers of little education in the developing countries are evidencing their willingness to change from traditional methods, once they are satisfied that a more profitable alternative is available. Generally speaking, conversion of the subsistence farmer to the new technology rests on four points. First, the alternative package of practices offered must be highly productive and profitable by comparison with his present system. Second, he must be shown, by demonstration, the proper way to use the technology and become convinced that he can carry this out. Third, the required inputs (fertilizer, seed, pesticide, credit) must be available to him when and where needed and at reasonable prices. And fourth, he must be assured of a satisfactory price and market for his harvested product at the time he plants and before he mortgages his future.

Extension services staffed with properly supported, mobile, production specialists can be of critical importance in agricultural production programs. But like the teacher, the investigator, and the farmer, the extension agent is only one link in the chain phenomenon of modernization of agriculture; there must be constant communication, continuity, and interaction so that new knowledge can be translated as quickly as possible into action for the benefit of the farmer. Over and over again, it has been shown that where this chain really functions effectively, the results can be dramatic, with multiple benefits to all concerned. Where the extension service is ill-served and poorly supported, however, this break in the chain can cause such a delay in the transmission of important materials and information that, until it is repaired, production levels improve only very slowly if at all.

PATTERN FOR SUCCESS

There is probably no single pattern for organizing the several components of agricultural production programs successfully and effectively; however, in the opinion of the authors, based on experience with The Rockefeller Foundation programs as well as observation of others, the following principles are essential for reasonably rapid and demonstrable progress.

First, the national needs should be carefully studied, commodity by commodity, and research and production goals established which are as ambitious as is consistent with sound science and the national interest of the country concerned.

Second, production-oriented research and training programs should be initiated, commodity by commodity, through the country's already existing institutions or through newly created institutions designed to become a part of the national fabric and to be financed by the country itself. Initially, the available technology should be tested for applicability; research efforts then can be concentrated on problems that still limit productivity.

Third, capable career scientists should be placed in charge of the programs, be given the technical and financial support needed, and then be allowed to continue their assignments for the substantial number of years required to achieve success. Short-term assignments of one or two years should be employed primarily to complement the efforts of career scientists responsible for progress.

Fourth, substantial numbers of young college graduates should be trained locally through internships of one to several years. By participating directly in the technical programs under the guidance of professionals, they can develop the skills, competence, and confidence needed to make them useful initially as research assistants and then as production specialists, extension agents, or employees of agricultural industry or government.

Fifth, the most outstanding of the men who benefit from internships should be given opportunities for advanced study to equip them for positions of leadership in their home research organizations, in governmental agencies, or in educational institutions.

Sixth, the government of the country concerned must be encouraged to treat agriculture as a basic industry through which economic development can be accelerated, to provide assured markets and incentive prices both for agricultural products and for the necessary industrial inputs, to provide credit at reasonable rates, to develop irrigation schemes in accordance with crop needs, and to strengthen the research, extension, and educational institutions that permit rapid and sustained progress.

Seventh, success of agricultural production efforts must be measured by the combined impact of research, education, and extension on the productivity and profitability of farming. Through organization of programs on a commodity basis, progress can be measured by increases in yields achieved on the experiment stations, then by cooperating farmers, and finally by the nation as a whole, in terms of average yields and total production.

Past Technical Assistance Programs

Evaluation of past programs for increasing food production has created both pessimism and optimism, depending on the program evaluated and the depth of the evaluation. Some programs certainly fell far short of attaining their objectives; others, however, have exceeded the original expectations. The reasons for the failures will be considered first, so that the section may end on an optimistic note with descriptions of some successes.

SOME PROBLEMS

It can be said, in general, that those programs that have ended in relative or complete failure have done so because their planners misunderstood the true nature of modern agriculture and ignored one or more of the essentials described earlier.

Some of the unsuccessful aid programs have placed too much emphasis on speed and visible results, often attempting to effect quick turn-arounds in economic conditions. In other instances, planners have unwisely pinned their hopes on the simple transfer of "know-how."

There also have been those who believed that the problem could be solved by a single remedy. One of the most widespread misconceptions has been the idea that the massive application of modern manufactured inputs—fertilizers, or pesticides, or machinery—to agricultural production in less-developed nations can quickly convert a pattern of underproduction to one of sufficiency. The fallacy of this belief as regards fertilizer use has long since been exposed. It is, of course, true that fertilizers, when joined to favorable combinations of soil, water, high-yielding varieties, and plant protection measures, do play an essential role in production, and that increased applications under such circumstances can pay substantial dividends. But the regular application of large amounts of fertilizer in the absence of these other factors has been demonstrated over and over again to be uneconomical and even, in some cases, to result in seriously reduced yields. In the same way, neither pesticides nor machinery should be relied on exclusively—and the list of mistaken single-remedy approaches is much longer, including irrigation, supply of credit, and provision of improved seeds. Each one of these is only a single component in a complex system, and used alone each one is of minimum value; their maximum value can be realized only when the several components are used in combination.

Other popular single panaceas have included "practical" training, the development of water resources, the organization or re-organization of extension services, comprehensive community development schemes, and the establishment of graduate institutions of education and research. Again, the advocates of these remedies failed to recognize that a combination of all these and many other components of a modern technological society is essential if agricultural production in the developing nations is to be substantially improved.

Sometimes, of course, it is claimed that programs failed because rural populations are beset with apathy, ignorance, and lack of enterprise. There is, however, ample evidence of the fallacy of this explanation. Rural populations are disadvantaged largely because they are remote, because they are not organized, and because they do not have the opportunities and the services enjoyed by urban dwellers who usually are more visible and more vocal concerning their needs. The rural areas often seem to be the last to receive critically important medical services, to be extended educational opportunities, and to be provided with other amenities and opportunities taken for granted in the cities. In spite of these disadvantages, not primarily of their own making, rural populations have over the centuries contributed mightily to the economies of their areas and could be vastly more productive if they were furnished the essential services and opportunities.

A second explanation, frequently offered, is that assistance efforts were defeated by the inequitable division of arable land among large landowners, small landholders, and tenants. Land reform is indeed needed in many of the poorer nations, and absentee-land-lordism has undoubtedly had a negative influence on agricultural production in these countries. Furthermore, in some parts of the world landlords are the only source of credit, which they often provide at usurious rates of interest, so that the almost defenseless tiller of the soil exists in a continual state of indebtedness tantamount to economic slavery. This situation is increasingly being recognized by the governments concerned. As populations expand and exert still heavier pressures on the land, it may be expected that greater attention will be paid to land reform and efforts made to assure that the available land is distributed and utilized to maximize the value of its productivity to the national economy. But the fact remains that agricultural improvement is not contingent on changes in the existing pattern of land distribution. Rather, it depends on well-conceived and well-executed action programs based on the essential components of research, education, and extension.

Today there are many agencies involved in international technical assistance. Some are multinational as exemplified by the Food and Agriculture Organization (FAO) of the United Nations, the United Nations Development Program (UNDP), the International Bank for Reconstruction and Development, the Inter-American Development Bank, the Asian Development Bank, and the Colombo Plan. Others are binational, such as the United States Agency for International Development (AID) and similar organizations in other countries. The private sector is represented by a number of projects involving corporate or business interests with national development schemes. Private philanthropy has been active for many years in cooperative programs with less-developed countries directed toward agricultural development, public health, education, and economic development, and there are many other agencies attempting in one way or another to contribute to the needs of the disadvantaged nations.

Foreign technical assistance and related forms of aid are difficult undertakings at best. In principle, it would appear most desirable that all such programs be multilateral to avoid the negative psychology sometimes created by the donor-receiver condition. Practically, however, to channel all efforts into multinational efforts is to assure the establishment of burgeoning bureaucracies with all of the complications, delays, and expediencies which would result. Experience teaches that it is clearly desirable to maintain the variety of programs in technical assistance while at the same time working toward closer cooperation among the several organizations for maximum progress toward common goals.

Both multinational and binational programs have been severely criticized by many as being confusing, ineffective, inconsistent, and rigidly bureaucratic. And most international technical assistance programs of whatever origin have at times been criticized by those who resent the necessity for receiving aid or who are supernationals or whose ideologies make them antagonistic to the donor agency or country. Nevertheless, it is believed that a fair appraisal would show that despite all of the problems attendant upon foreign technical assistance and all of the mistakes which have been made and the failures which have been so often reported and magnified, the total effect has been beneficial to millions of the world's disadvantaged. The important goal for the future is improved communication and understanding, better coordination and cooperation, and ever-increasing efficiency in the progress toward well-conceived and well-defined goals.

SUCCESSFUL PROGRAMS

It would be impossible to attempt to describe any major proportion of the accomplishments of technical assistance programs, but a few general statements plus certain case histories might serve to illustrate possibilities of this type of international collaboration for economic development.

Over the years, FAO has been a central force in creating our present awareness of the nature and seriousness of the world food problem. This organization has provided guidance to a great many countries on a multitude of problems related to agricultural development. Prominent programs include an international plant disease survey, the cataloging of varieties of food crops, continuing studies of land economics, international task forces dealing with the production of basic commodities, and a training program for younger agricultural scientists. FAO continues to stimulate highly useful international exchanges of technical and economic information, and has begun to press for much needed cooperative international research. Working closely with the UNDP, FAO has arranged for the financing of national agricultural research and development projects in many countries and has often provided critical technical assistance to these national or regional efforts.

The international development banks have been of enormous benefit in stimulating and supporting soundly conceived projects directed to economic development in many countries. By extending both 15- to 20-year loans at standard commercial rates and 50-year credits at no interest—called International Development Association credits—these organizations have bolstered local economies and provided critical support at times and places where most needed. Their activities are many and varied. They have contributed vastly and significantly to improving transportation, providing new power sources, building important industrial plants for the manufacture of agricultural chemicals, and supporting fundamental projects dealing with agricultural research in educational institutions. Certainly the international banks have become a powerful force for balanced development in the emerging nations and have proved to be a unique instrumentality for furthering economic progress.

United States bilateral foreign assistance began with the Point Four announcement of 1949 and the establishment of the Technical Cooperation Administration in 1950. Since that time, our overseas aid program has undergone several reorganizations and is currently administered by the Agency for International Development, AID. During the almost two decades of its existence, the program has provided assistance to developing countries throughout the world.

It was perhaps inevitable, because of the size and ambitious nature of the U.S. aid program that the agencies responsible for its administration sometimes tended to become large, often unwieldy, organizations with bureaucratic tendencies. Given a gigantic task, successive changes in leadership and a variety of political pressures, it was to be expected that there would be both successes and failures and that the latter would attract more attention than the former. It was hoped that each reorganization, based on past experience, would improve performance. However, over the years, many of the restrictions persisted and the funds in 1968 requested for the AID program were drastically reduced by Congressional action.

AID has many successes to its credit and has established a variety of projects in agriculture which have been demonstrably effective. A few examples include: a bold and successful project in Turkey to increase spring-wheat production; "Operation Spread" in the Philippines which has helped that country to become self-sufficient in rice; and a highly effective corn production campaign in Kenya financed through the U.S. Department of Agriculture. Similar successes in Latin America could be cited.

The U.S. business sector has also become increasingly interested in overseas cooperation. Participants include seed companies, chemical and machinery manufacturers, construction firms, mining and mineral corporations, oil companies, and food processors. An Agribusiness Council has been established to deal with and coordinate certain overseas activities of American business, and a number of representative groups have formed associations for the purpose of contributing to economic development overseas.

One of the most notable institutional inventions in support of agriculture has been the land-grant college. Over the years, these uniquely American creations have been central to the success of the U.S. agricultural industry. Combining education, research, and extension, land-grant universities serve the people of this nation in an extraordinary fashion. They have led in raising the standards of agricultural practice and production to unprecedented levels. Land-grant universities have learned to work with farmers, the agricultural industries, political leadership, and other segments of society in such ways as to provide continuing development of the entire agricultural sector with demonstrable and increasing benefit for all Americans. Because of their successes it was natural that the land-grant universities would be asked to work overseas with sister universities abroad and because of their nature it was to be expected that they would respond with understanding and enthusiasm. Supported principally by AID but to an extent by foundations and other private organizations, and on occasions without special support, many of our land-grant colleges have formed associations abroad which have resulted in substantial and visible progress. Perhaps the improvement of the educational process and curriculum has been a major thrust, but research and extension have not been neglected in attempting to bring about the development of sound agricultural programs abroad. As more of the agricultural institutons in the developing countries offer programs similar in type and quality, but tailored to the local scene, they can largely satisfy the scientific manpower requirements for agricultural development.

As illustrative of successful national agricultural production programs we have chosen certain cooperative efforts of The Rockefeller Foundation because we know them best and they have been in effect over a sufficient period of time to permit an evaluation. These efforts have from the beginning been focused on selected goals; their nature has been based on principles established in the 1940's; practices employed have continuously evolved as the Foundation expanded its efforts both geographically and conceptually. The programs reported herein are offered as case histories to show that our optimism with reference to the possibilities of major increases in agricultural production is based on experience rather than theory.

The Mexican Agricultural Program—In the early 1940's, Mexico faced the absolute necessity of sharply increasing average yields of its basic food crops, if the national food supplies were to keep pace with the rapidly growing population. To the leadership of the country it seemed clear that Mexico would need some outside help in solving its agricultural problems. Accordingly, The Rockefeller Foundation was invited to cooperate with Mexican governmental leaders and scientific personnel in a campaign to close the food gap, with particular reference to the country's two basic food cereals— corn and wheat.

The Foundation accepted this challenge as its first attempt at a practical program of agricultural production that could lead to improved nutrition for an entire nation. Beginning in 1943, a small cadre of Foundation agricultural scientists was assigned to Mexico (ultimately the number reached twenty), and these men at once began working with their Mexican colleagues to identify the bottlenecks to production and to determine the means of removing them.

It was quickly discovered that soil management systems in Mexico were generally inadequate, that water was often a limiting factor, that pests and diseases annually took heavy tolls, and that the varieties of wheat and corn in current use were of low productive capacity. It was evident also that agricultural education was substandard; graduates lacked field experience in technical agriculture and the numbers being turned out each year by the country's agricultural schools were woefully insufficient. There was no organized extension service; research on agricultural problems was inadequate to satisfy the requirements of the country; fertilizers were not only expensive but also not readily available; and pesticides were lacking.

This catalogue of problems might have seemed insurmountable, but no single problem by itself was insoluble, nor was it an impossible task to tackle the several problems as a group. In fact, it was recognized that a succession of single solutions, one following the other, could not quickly increase Mexico's production of food grains. Rather, progress must be sought on all fronts simultaneously. Results would then be synergistic, their effect in combination adding up to much more than the sum of their individual effects.

As expected, initial progress was slow. It was first necessary to reach an accommodation permitting all elements of the pattern to function together smoothly and comfortably; reservations had to be overcome, friendships formed, and close working relationships developed. At the same time, it was necessary to establish new procedures. A modern program of research and its application as well as a training program had to be started at once so that competent young Mexican scientists, in increasing numbers, could participate in all aspects of the work and ultimately assume responsibility for its leadership and direction.

During the early period of this cooperative venture, education and learning took place on both sides. The Mexicans had much to teach their American counterparts, and certainly The Rockefeller Foundation group had knowledge and experience useful to their Mexican colleagues. Everyone involved was conscious of the program's tremendous importance for the future of Mexico's agriculture, and all other concerns were subordinated to this end. The scientific problems were many and complicated, but although work toward their solution was laborious and difficult, it was at the same time rewarding.

In the early 1940's, Mexico's average yields of wheat and corn were so low that any improvement, however slight, would automatically benefit the entire economy. The national average wheat yield was only 11.5 bushels per acre. Maize production averaged a pitifully low eight bushels per acre, or about a fifth of the average then being achieved in the U.S. Corn Belt.

First efforts involved worldwide collection of genetic materials. Corn and wheat varieties from all over the world were brought together, tested in field trials, and the elite varieties chosen for use in the research and improvement program. This required a vast amount of field work, something which was unusual in Mexico at that time. However, once it was understood that this exercise represented the essential means of obtaining solid information on which to base a continuing research program, everyone did his part cheerfully and efficiently.

The major technical limitations to production were soon identified. All the wheat varieties then being grown in Mexico were highly susceptible to a series of races of black stem rust as well as to other diseases. They struggled through moisture-deficient seasons on impoverished soils, and the use of fertilizers resulted in production of overly luxuriant foliage, lodging (falling over) of the plants, and disappointing grain yields.

With corn, the situation was highly complex: there existed in

Mexico literally thousands of varieties, each of them having become specifically adapted over the centuries to a particular set of environmental conditions and to a specific cropping season, and each representing a particular grain type preferred by inhabitants of the locality. Most of the corn varieties were being grown on soils depleted by thousands of years of continuous cropping; some relatively productive types were cultivated in a few, still-fertile valleys, but these were of limited use elsewhere because of their special daylength and temperature requirements and their specific growing seasons. Primitive and diminutive popcorns were found in valleys and on hillsides at altitudes of a mile and a half, while robust soft-dent types grew along the tropical coasts. White grain was generally preferred for tortillas, though yellow to orange-red flint varieties prevailed in some coastal areas.

Even under the best local treatment and conditions, the existing wheat and corn varieties were unable to produce the high yields which were needed and which would make profitable the use of fertilizers, machinery, and other inputs of modern agriculture. Therefore, it became necessary to identify elite material from whatever source, make sure of its adaptability, and recombine this material with other varieties that could contribute important characteristics—such as high yielding ability, disease resistance, satisfactory grain type, and resistance to lodging. The resulting thousands of new strains then had to be tested on a regional basis, and the best of them further refined and grown in yield tests before they were considered ready for release as improved varieties. This process is long, laborious, and highly sophisticated, requiring great care and a tremendous amount of record-keeping as well as constant attention to the interaction with the other aspects of modern agricultural production; it must be guided by capable and properly trained scientists.

As improved, adapted, disease- and pest-resistant varieties were developed, information had to be obtained on the proper way to manage them on the farm so that they would achieve their potential. This involved appropriate dates and rates and depths of seeding, the most efficient utilization of water, whether rainfall, irrigation, or both, proper types and rates and timing of fertilizer applications to assure that the varieties were properly nourished, and on occasion the use of pesticides and herbicides as collateral accelerators in the total production pattern.

As results began to accrue in the combined research and training program, the time arrived for utilizing the improved materials in practical fashion, that is, in the farmers' fields. In the absence of an extension service, the task of educating the farmers in the use of the new varieties had to be undertaken by the program. Several different methods were used: the planting of improved varieties in the fields alongside the older varieties so that farmers could make their own comparisons; the establishment of demonstration plots on a regional basis; the inauguration of a series of so-called "field days" at which farmers were brought together at experiment stations and substations to see for themselves what could be accomplished in their own area by using their customary methods with certain readily available improvements. Farmers also were encouraged to attend agricultural fairs where they could view demonstrations of new materials both in living form and in pictures, filmstrips, and movies. Finally, program staff participated directly in community meetings in many parts of the country in order to explain the nature of the research and its purposes and to try to convince listeners of its potential economic value to themselves and their families. Simultaneously, better farmers were encouraged to become producers of seed for the commercial market.

* * *

From the beginning, great care was taken to assure that Mexican leadership at all levels was kept completely informed as to the work in progress. As stated earlier, Mexican scientific and administrative personnel were involved in every step of the process, from the initial field work to the final conclusion of the experiments. The results were published in various forms expected to be useful to scientists, government leaders, extension agents, and some farmers. Continuous effort was made to encourage government leadership to put more and more support behind agricultural education and research and its application, to expand and improve irrigation facilities, and to provide favorable terms of farm trade. Ultimately, more than 700 young Mexicans served as interns in the research program; and under a fellowship and scholarship program established by The Rockefeller Foundation, a number of these young scientists were enabled to go abroad for advanced study (Mexico not yet having its own graduate school of agriculture). In collaboration with the Government of Mexico, these specialists, on their return, were placed in positions of responsibility so that they could contribute their share to the total advance of the country's agricultural production.

Mexican scientists responded enthusiastically to the increased opportunities to work effectively and to improve their professional status. Slowly but steadily their numbers grew and they could take on a larger share of the work. An extension service was organized along with an information service, and thus gradually full momentum was achieved in a well-conceived agricultural development plan leading to increased production of basic food grains.

A number of other agricultural improvement projects were initiated and then spun off the central effort as it developed. These involved work with beans, potatoes, vegetables, sorghum, soybeans, forage and pasture crops, and, ultimately, poultry. The purpose was to multiply the value of the experience gained in the early days of the program by putting it to use in new contexts, principally under the leadership of outstanding young Mexican agricultural scientists. This hoped-for "multiplier" effect was satisfactorily realized.

* * *

This cooperative venture begun in the early 1940's between the Government of Mexico and The Rockefeller Foundation soon yielded concrete results. By 1955, Mexico had closed its food gap in the production of both corn and wheat and had additional quantities of other food and related basic crops to meet national needs. By 1968, national average wheat yields exceeded 40 bushels an acre or almost quadruple the 11.5-bushel average in 1943; corn yields were double those of 25 years earlier; potato production was more than triple that of 1950; and major gains had been recorded with other crops. And it must be realized that this conversion of national corn and wheat deficits into surpluses took place while Mexico's population was doubling; had the program been geared only to closing the gap between food and population that existed in 1943, the country's present population would still lack adequate supplies of the basic foods. Today, however, Mexico has the biological material, the technology, the leadership, and the scientific direction to adjust production of corn and wheat to its own requirements and keep this in balance with the national agricultural production pattern.

The cooperative program, having served its purpose, was formally succeeded in 1961 by an all-Mexican National Institute for Agricultural Research, with responsibility for investigating the wide variety of important agricultural problems still unsolved and for applying research results wherever needed to increase production. The Institute is administered, staffed, and led by highly qualified Mexican scientists who are making significant contributions to the national economy with each succeeding year.

* * *

Although the objectives of the cooperative program in Mexico were formally limited to that country's needs, the Foundation early recognized that information acquired in Mexico should immediately be made available to other Latin American countries and that the best way to accomplish this was to allow young scientists from these countries to participate in the program, become familiar with all its aspects, and then return home to stimulate creation of similar centers. Accordingly, a number of young Latin Americans—from Ecuador, Peru, Brazil, and Colombia—were given scholarships to work with the team in Mexico.

At the same time, established scientists from these and other Latin American countries representing a number of disciplines were invited to visit the Mexican program, and arrangements were made to provide information and materials on a continuing basis so that as innovations were established in Mexico, they could be tested elsewhere.

In addition, Foundation scientists assigned to the Mexican program frequently visited other Latin American countries to consult with the local scientific and political leaders, to select scholars and fellows for advanced training in Mexico or in the United States, and to be helpful in every way possible. One result of these visits was the establishment of a cooperative Central American Corn Improvement Program, which was subsequently expanded to include subtropical food crops like beans and sorghums, and tropical forages.

National Improvement Programs in Colombia, Chile, and India —By the late 1940's the progress being made in Mexico had begun to attract worldwide attention, with the result that The Rockefeller Foundation received numerous invitations from the governments of other countries to set up programs of research leading to improvements in the production of basic food crops.

In 1950, an agreement was signed with the Government of Colombia, establishing a second cooperative program. Under distinguished Colombian political leadership and with outstanding collaboration from the nation's scientists, this program has since achieved major progress in increasing production of barley, wheat, corn, potatoes, and other food crops. Equally important, the program has resulted in the establishment of the semi-autonomous Colombian Institute of Agriculture, which is concerned not only with all aspects of agricultural research and extension, but also with graduate agricultural education in collaboration with the National University of Colombia.

In 1955, the Foundation embarked on its third national venture in Latin America when it agreed to cooperate with the Government of Chile on the improvement and utilization of new varieties of winter and spring wheats, of the forage crops with which these rotate, and in soil management. Here again, it can be reported that a successful program led to the development of a national Agricultural Research Institute, with modern experiment stations near Santiago and Temuco, and staffed by able Chileans.

The year 1956 marked the Foundation's initial attempt to cooperate with an Asian country in agricultural improvement. In that year it agreed to help in establishing a cooperative agricultural research and demonstration program on corn in India, involving both national and state agencies and institutions, and to assist with the strengthening of the Indian Agricultural Research Institute in New Delhi. Subsequently, this program was expanded to include sorghums, millets, wheat, and rice, the improvement of experiment station facilities, the development of seed production and distribution capabilities, and the strengthening of supporting work in plant pathology, entomology, soils, and economics. Today, India has become a research and training center benefiting a number of other countries with similar conditions.

Assistance to Institutions of Higher Education—The point has already been made that, in each of its cooperative national programs, The Rockefeller Foundation has sought to improve the given country's institutions of higher education, so that year by year these could play a greater and more leading part in the preparation of youth for increasingly important careers in agricultural sciences. In Mexico, the Foundation participated in undergraduate agricultural education and also joined with Mexican leaders in establishing at Chapingo the first graduate school of agriculture in the country, and at Monterrey a postgraduate school of agriculture at the Institute of Technology. Collateral support has been given over the years to colleges of agriculture and veterinary medicine in Colombia, Peru, Brazil, Chile, Nigeria, Sudan, India, the Philippines, and Thailand. In every instance, these efforts were accompanied by a fellowship program designed to produce larger numbers of qualified and dedicated scientists able to take leadership positions in the institutions concerned.

Development of Research Networks—As the Foundation's agricultural activities expanded southward in Latin America and eastward to India, its scientists constantly endeavored to extend any success they might have to still other countries. For example, as soon as corn germplasm collections had been evaluated in Mexico, every effort was made to send small quantities to other parts of the world to be tested under local conditions. If it was discovered that some of these diverse strains had certain advantages over the indigenous types, plans were made to build them into breeding programs for adaptation to the local environment. The same was done with wheat, and subsequently with other crops. Soon there developed a two-way flow, the central program in Mexico sending information and materials to new areas and the local experiment stations and scientists in return sending to Mexico information and materials of their own that would be helpful in future experimentation and research.

Much has already been accomplished through these international networks of cooperative activities in agriculture, as will be discussed in the next section. But more such networks are needed. This mechanism offers international agencies an outstanding opportunity to promote collaboration among nations in a wide spectrum of useful activities from which the participating countries could gain immensely.

Internationalization of Efforts

In recent decades there has been much talk about internationalism. In many phases of agricultural improvement, an international viewpoint is absolutely essential to progress, because the problems themselves are not limited by political boundaries. Control of many migratory insects and wind-borne plant-disease organisms, for example, requires coordinated effort on the part of many nations and the better the coordination, the more effective the control. In the same way, the greater the internationalization of efforts to improve agriculture in the food-deficit countries, the sooner can these countries achieve self-sufficiency.

SYNERGISM OF PROGRAMS

Any new national production programs being established today should be able to take advantage of the fact that a substantial number of such efforts already are under way in all of the agricultural regions of the world. It should be unnecessary now for any country to have to "start from scratch" and go through laborious and slow stages of development to reach the goal of increased production. The experience gained in past programs, the lessons learned, the materials produced, and the success achieved should all constitute a short cut to progress, assuming that the national leadership understands the country's problems and the urgent need for tackling them directly and promptly.

Tremendous opportunities thus exist for achieving a synergism of national and international efforts, so that important information, materials, and manpower can rapidly be made available to help in the establishment of new programs, assuring balanced, continuing progress on all fronts. This already has been partly achieved through the device of international research and training centers.

CATALYTIC INTERNATIONAL CENTERS

Description of the centers now in operation, or authorized by several cooperating agencies, will best be understood if their role is first explained in general terms.

International centers should serve as the catalysts of collaboration in research efforts, as the hubs of networks of needed activity. Their establishment permits the quick creation of truly interdisciplinary teams of highly capable scientists who bring their talents to bear as rapidly as possible on technical problems of greatest importance in the economic development of the regions served. In addition, however, such centers insure continuity of effort on problems for the number of years required for solution. The depth of the research undertaken at a center is therefore greater than would be possible for some time to come in newly established national institutions. International centers also bring together and facilitate the rapid exchange of useful information and materials, and, of particular importance, offer further education and training to the specialists who will in turn initiate and expand the indispensable national programs.

The government of a center by an international board of trustees furthermore assures that the research and training objectives continually match the wider and most urgent needs of society. And, as men of stature in their own nations, the trustees are able to facilitate arrangements for needed cooperative work.

Finally, because of their non-profit status the international centers are eligible for support, either through grants or contracts, from the full range of interested individuals and organizations wishing to assist. To sum up, they allow the problems to be brought together with the funds and talent needed for their solution.

THE INTERNATIONAL RICE RESEARCH INSTITUTE

Recognizing that rapid improvement in the quantity and quality of tropical rice, the staple food of vast millions of people in the "rice bowl" of Asia, would represent a major contribution to increased world food supplies, the Ford and Rockefeller Foundations in 1961 jointly founded the International Rice Research Institute (IRRI), located at Los Baños, close to the College of Agriculture of the University of the Philippines. Initially, The Ford Foundation contributed the funds for construction and equipment of the Institute, and The Rockefeller Foundation undertook to provide the scientific staff and to underwrite operating costs. Subsequently, as the IRRI program moved more rapidly than had been anticipated, the two foundations agreed to contribute equally to its core support, and this continues to be the situation, although other agencies such as AID and the Government of the Philippines have also contributed financially. The latter Government, in addition, acts as host to the Institute and has facilitated its establishment, and Philippine scientific and related entities collaborate with it. An autonomous, non-profit enterprise, IRRI has an international board of trustees and a staff of qualified and dedicated agricultural scientists recruited from Australia, Ceylon, India, Japan, Pakistan, the Philippines, Taiwan, Thailand, and the United States.

Immediately on the Institute's establishment, the research staff set about studying all aspects of the rice plant—its nature, behavior, and requirements—in an effort to learn everything possible relating to its productivity. Beginning with a large collection of rice strains and varieties from all over the world, geneticists, physiologists, soil scientists, pathologists, entomologists, and others joined in this major interdisciplinary research effort. They quickly identified most of the technical factors blocking high yields in tropical Asia. There was an obvious requirement, as demonstrated with wheat in Mexico and with rice in temperate-zone Japan, for varieties having short stiff straw and fewer erect leaves so that plants could more efficiently utilize light and nutrients for production of grain rather than of foliage. Insensitivity to photoperiod was also required to allow planting of rice at any time of the year and over a greater geographical area. In addition, there was urgent need for grain dormancy, to prevent sprouting of the seed before harvest during rainy periods; for genetic resistance to the diverse races of the rice blast disease; for chemical control of the devastating rice stem borer while a search for genetic resistance was under way; and for information about rates and dates of planting, rates and timing of fertilizer application, and other factors that would contribute to high grain production per hectare per day.

With these requirements in mind, IRRI set about creating rice varieties tailored to meet the climatic and other conditions existing in the various "rice bowl" countries. Through careful selection, testing, and recombination, it proved possible to produce a superior type of tropical rice within four years. The first released variety was IR8, popularly known as "miracle rice" in much of Southeast Asia because of its tremendously increased yield over that of traditional varieties when grown with high levels of fertilizer application. IR8 is a dwarf type, with short, stiff straw: it effectively utilizes large amounts of fertilizer in grain production but is resistant to lodging; it is resistant also to a number of the major pests and diseases of rice. When grown with newly developed management techniques and at high levels of fertilizer application, it can produce yields two to four times those achieved with previously available varieties and methods.

With its release to growers during the summer of 1966, IR8 was sent to many rice-producing areas and soon was being extensively grown in the Philippines, Indonesia, Malaysia, Ceylon, Burma, Pakistan, India, and Thailand. It also was introduced into several regions of Africa and Latin America. According to a rough estimate, within 30 months the value of the increased rice produced from this new dwarf type had exceeded $300 million annually.

The International Rice Research Institute has working relation-

ships with all of the above countries and with FAO and is attempting to develop a network of interconnected rice research centers so
that the materials developed at IRRI can readily be made available
in each country. Ultimately, it is hoped that this network can become a worldwide effort—interconnected and intercommunicated,
with international exchanges of material and personnel—to insure
as rapid an increase in world rice production as possible.

Besides its research program, IRRI has a vigorous and active
education and training program. Young agricultural scientists come
from many countries for a period of residence and study at the
Institute. After they return to their own countries, they continue
their friendships, remain in professional contact, and cooperate actively in common goals. The average number of in-service, or intern,
trainees at any one time at Los Baños is between 65 and 75. Depending on their individual circumstance, trainees remain at the Institute from one to two years.

THE INTERNATIONAL CORN AND WHEAT IMPROVEMENT CENTER

The International Corn and Wheat Improvement Center
(CIMMYT, from its Spanish name), with headquarters in Mexico,
evolved from The Rockefeller Foundation's earlier cooperative
work in Latin America. Like IRRI, it is supported jointly by the
Ford and Rockefeller Foundations, is an autonomous institute, and
has an international board of trustees and an international staff of
scientists. CIMMYT both conducts fundamental research on corn
and wheat and assists improvement efforts related to these two basic
cereals in all parts of the world where they are important to human
nutrition. Representatives of CIMMYT travel widely to discuss
problems of mutual interest with other scientists, and cooperative
relationships are maintained with interested countries in Latin
America, Asia, and East and West Africa; recently this network of
communication has been expanded to include the countries of the
Near East.

As would be expected, the CIMMYT program also makes provision for foreign scientists to come to Mexico and be directly associated with the research activities for a time. Intensive studies are

under way on all aspects of the corn and the wheat plants—their morphology, physiology, resistance to diseases and insect pests, length-of-day reaction, responses to fertilizer, and many others—in an attempt, through biological engineering, to produce the "super varieties" which can be the hope of the future.

That many of the superior, high-yielding wheat varieties developed in Mexico, both before and after the advent of CIMMYT, are excellently adapted for growing in a wide range of other countries has already been clearly demonstrated. Likewise, elite complexes of corn germplasm assembled in Mexico are proving valuable in a number of national production programs, not only when combined with indigenous material but also when used directly without such blending.

In the mid-1960's, CIMMYT was instrumental in helping to narrow the food gap in Asia. It has contributed the technology and training underlying the markedly successful wheat production efforts of India and Afghanistan. For its program in Pakistan, it has received special support from The Ford Foundation. This extraordinarily important venture in Pakistan is under the technical leadership of an eminent Mexican scientist who participated as an "intern" in the original cooperative agricultural program in Mexico; subsequently, on fellowships, he earned his master's and Ph.D. degrees at United States institutions, and then returned home to become the first Mexican director of his country's wheat improvement work. The Pakistan program rapidly established local centers at which superior wheat and corn materials from CIMMYT and other sources could be received, tested in competition with other varieties, blended into local varieties when necessary, and ultimately produced on a large scale under improved management.

TROPICAL CENTERS

Having previously joined forces in establishing the International Rice Research Institute, the two foundations have recently decided to collaborate in creating two additional international research centers—dedicated in this instance to acquiring greater scientific knowledge regarding the tropics, for the purpose of putting vast unused or under-utilized lands there to work in the service of world agriculture. Of these two new centers, the one in the Western Hemisphere has now been formally established in Colombia—the International Center for Tropical Agriculture (CIAT, from its Spanish name). It has responsibility for studying both crop and animal production and receives support from the Ford, Rockefeller, and Kellogg Foundations. (The latter foundation has also long been active and effective in medical education, nutrition, and agricultural extension in Latin America.) The Eastern Hemisphere center, the International Institute of Tropical Agriculture, established in Nigeria with initial support from the Ford and Rockefeller Foundations, is intended to emphasize work on tropical crops and soils.

Surveys indicate that for a variety of reasons, great expanses of land in the tropics, particularly in lowland tropical areas of Latin America, Africa, and Asia, are either still far below their potential in food production, or else have not yet been exploited in this respect. Some of the existing problems stem from nutrient deficiencies in the soils, some from the fact that crops and animals in these areas are attacked the year round by disease organisms and insect pests that multiply rapidly under the prevailing conditions of continuous high temperature and humidity. As water control and water supply present further problems, and certain of the major lowland tropical areas have also remained remote and uncomfortable for human habitation, development of adapted, high-yielding crop varieties and animal strains has inevitably received minimal, if any, attention. But with present advances in air transportation and in bridge and road construction, the ease of long-distance connection by radio and television, and air-conditioning and power units, these regions can rapidly become more accessible and comfortable to human beings. Given the benefits of fundamental and then adaptive agricultural research, certain of these areas should quickly become major centers of food and fiber production. And it may be noted that yields per acre per year in these areas might far exceed those of temperate-climate areas because of the 365-day growing season in the tropics.

These international tropical centers are therefore dedicated to the general task of making tropical areas more livable and more productive. That they can accomplish more by concerted international effort than could be achieved by individual national endeavors seems certain from the record of the centers already in operation.

VALUE ILLUSTRATED BY WHEAT

The potential value of all international crop improvement efforts can be well illustrated by the concrete accomplishments of the international wheat program, which are now clearly visible and easily measurable. The basis was laid in Mexico with the development of varieties of wheat highly resistant to rust, smuts, and other diseases, well adapted to various soil conditions, insensitive to length of day, and highly responsive to fertilizer and resistant to lodging—in brief, exceedingly efficient in the production of grain. These semi-dwarf varieties have firm, stiff straw, short height, and a high ratio of grain to straw; and because of their short, stiff straw, they stand up well under conditions of excess moisture, fertilizer, and wind. These varieties were initially responsible for helping to close the food gap in Mexico, have since contributed to increased food production elsewhere in Latin America, and are now being utilized on a vast and increasing scale in India, Pakistan, Turkey, Afghanistan, and in other nations where spring wheats can be grown.

The recent improvement of wheat production in Asia is a dramatic story. Preliminary surveys in India and Pakistan strongly indicated that improved varieties developed in Mexico might be successful in these countries also and hence might provide the basis for wheat improvement and production programs. The Governments of India and Pakistan, therefore, boldly proceeded in 1966–67 to purchase large quantities of the new wheat seed, as produced by commercial farmers in Mexico, and then carefully selected, tested, cleaned, and packaged. During the 1966 and 1967 seasons, a total of 58,000 tons was purchased from Mexico by India and Pakistan to accelerate their seed-increase and ultimately wheat-increase programs. In addition, 22,000 tons were purchased in 1967 by Turkey. Within two years, India had planted the new wheat seed on nearly 7,000,000 acres, or 20 per cent of the country's total wheat acreage;

Pakistan had planted about 3,000,000 acres, or 30 per cent of its total wheat acreage. The national average yield in India in 1968 was about 1300 kilograms per hectare, or about 500 kilograms above the 800 kilogram average for the period 1962–65. It is estimated that the performance of the new wheats in Pakistan was at least as good as in India. In the coastal areas of Turkey, where simultaneously 18,000 tons of new seed were planted, the resulting yields were estimated at almost three times the national average.

Never before in history has there been such an undertaking. The risks are great, but the potential future gains for hungry humanity make these well worth taking, and the most serious risks are being minimized by continuous adaptive research.

Improved varieties of corn, sorghums, millets, and rice are now likewise becoming available in increased quantity. Like wheat, they are contributing in major and significant fashion to increased food supplies in certain major areas of production and will ultimately find their way to other areas. This is positive evidence of what can be done by adaptive research, rapid dissemination of improved materials, and their wise and prompt utilization under proper conditions for the benefit of local agricultural production.

Hope for the Future

ATTITUDES ARE IMPROVING

We believe that man can soon subsist himself more easily and adequately, provided he acts with intelligence and determination to systematize and internationalize his efforts toward that goal. This belief is based on the growing awareness of the nature of the food problem, evidence that major gains can be achieved in the productivity of conventional agriculture, and the recent dramatic success of crop production campaigns in some developing nations.

Most countries now want to modernize their agriculture. Their leaders are recognizing the multiple factors involved and are showing willingness to make the necessary efforts. In many of the less-developed nations, of course, some outside help will be needed;

but the growing realization that each country must have the desire for progress, backed with the resolve to do all it can to ensure success of improvement programs, is at least a hopeful sign.

There also is hope in the fact that foreign aid agencies now have more knowledge, improved plant materials, and technology to transmit to the less-developed countries—and even greater hope in the fact that this transmission is being made effectively in a number of populous countries. Moreover, research is continually producing new information, better techniques, and improved biological materials of value in agricultural systems.

PROMISING RESEARCH DEVELOPMENTS

Since improvements in agriculture inevitably trace back to advances in the basic sciences, continuation of fundamental research is essential. No single science holds the key to agricultural development; it has been the interaction and application of findings in mathematics, physics, chemistry, and biology that have allowed some parts of the world to reach levels of agricultural productivity not contemplated as recently as 1940. Significantly, in regions of highest average productivity, rates of gain are still accelerating.

In the plant sciences, the origins of major species and their relatives are receiving scattered attention and much of the wealth of germplasm has been collected, although it largely remains to be systematically evaluated and exploited. With advances in genetics, more effective and rapid techniques of breeding are being identified, and specific genes for useful characters are being located and their modes of inheritance determined. In crop physiology, attention is only beginning to be focused on the "architecture" of crop plants as this affects efficiency in the utilization of light and nutrients for the production of harvestable product; interdisciplinary efforts are needed here, involving plant breeders, geneticists, physiologists, biochemists, soil physicists, and engineers.

A recent development of great consequence is the incorporation of insensitivity to photoperiod into rice, wheat, and potentially in sorghum; with the flowering mechanism uninfluenced by day-length, geographical adaptation is greatly extended. More importantly, with tropical crops such as rice, year-round planting and harvest becomes feasible with controlled water supply; consequently, there is a more uniform flow of product into the market throughout the year, prices are stabilized, and the requirement for storage facilities reduced. This feature has yet to be provided in varieties of many important tropical crops, particularly corn and soybeans.

Progress is being made in the chemical control of flowering which allows harvest of some crops to be scheduled, and hormones are being increasingly utilized to influence plant growth in ways useful to man.

Plant pathologists and entomologists have combined their skills with those of plant breeders and geneticists to develop plant species that have higher levels of resistance to major pests and pathogens than do their prototypes. Disease resistance is obtained most effectively through protoplasmic change, and more attention is being given to the innumerable opportunities for development in this direction, particularly through international cooperation. At the same time, the combined efforts of pathologists, chemists, and entomologists have resulted in a whole series of highly efficient chemical compounds capable of protecting plants from pests and pathogens that can cause severe decreases in yields or even total crop loss. Inorganic compounds with a high degree of protective efficiency are now available, as well as "systemic" compounds that operate from within the host tissues; these may be either synthesized organic compounds or antibiotic substances extracted from other plants or animals, but principally from microorganisms.

Prospects are good that the cereal grains and other crops will one day have much higher levels of protein of greater nutritive value, which could be of world importance in combating widespread dietary protein deficiency.

With the combined contributions from genetics, plant physiology, plant pathology, and entomology, highly productive and widely adapted new varieties will become increasingly available, biologically engineered to make optimum use of light, nutrients, and water. On another front, varieties are being specifically tailored for mechanical harvest, even of such unlikely crops as tomatoes, grapes, and cucumbers.

Wide crosses, among crop species and even genera, are becoming more feasible with more detailed knowledge of genetics and techniques of tissue culture.

In the animal field, similar progress is taking place. Nutrition is being rapidly improved, providing dramatically higher rates of gain and reducing markedly the time required for animals to reach market weights. Breeding systems have been designed to permit production of hybrid poultry and to increase efficiency of production of large animals. Use of antibiotics and supplements in feedstuffs and of highly effective and specific vaccines contribute to health and vitality of animals.

Research is revealing several ways in which urgent needs for protein may be met. Of particular importance is that biochemists, geneticists, and plant breeders should soon produce cereal grain varieties having greater proportions of protein with properly balanced quantities of essential amino acids. Grain legumes are especially good sources of protein of high quality, but additional research is necessary to increase their productivity and to develop varieties and associated cropping practices for the many regions where yields are low or where such crops are not yet grown. Available technology already permits high productivity of poultry and swine in almost any climate. By improvement of forage crops and pastures, and with adequate health protection for animals, production of beef and dairy products can be substantially increased on vast areas not well suited for cultivated crops. But, for many people suffering from dietary protein deficiency, particularly families with young children, adequate nutrition can only occur as disposable income is increased to permit the purchase of nutritious foods. For rural families, this can occur only through greater production of salable farm products.

Knowledge gained in the basic and applied sciences has permitted great progress in the manufacture of nitrogenous fertilizers, with accompanying reductions in cost; consequently, work has accelerated on the use of very high levels of fertilizer for crop production, not only with food crops but also with forage and pasture crops for animal feeding.

Prospects are brightening for food production in arid coastal regions, particularly through food factories associated with conventional or nuclear. "power packages" that would permit desalinization of sea water for irrigation or for production of food crops in enclosed systems.

Particularly promising opportunities exist for development of flourishing agricultural systems for large areas in the humid tropics, especially in South America and Africa. And, by incorporation of greater winter hardiness in plant species, it should be possible to extend crop and animal production in the colder regions of the world.

But perhaps the most hopeful development of all is the striking progress being made through conventional agriculture in raising food production levels in the vast areas already under cultivation where yields have remained low for centuries.

AN OPTIMISTIC OUTLOOK

In this discussion we have placed emphasis on the potential for increased food production but have also stressed the fact that the potential cannot be converted into actuality without intelligent, coordinated, and persistent efforts. Man has created the potential; many men will determine the actual values that emerge from it.

The strictly technical aspects of agricultural improvement are reasonably well understood by a small number of scientists. Given the availability of individuals fully qualified to understand and attack the problems of production through the scientific method, it is possible in almost any nation to bring about improvements of real significance. The accomplishments already recorded by a number of the developing countries are adequate evidence of what others can do. They demonstrate clearly and beyond doubt that the quality and the quantity of basic foodstuffs can be improved through research and its adaptation, if reinforced by the supporting services and the supply of manufactured inputs so essential to the success of a modern agricultural industry.

Of course, there always are obstacles to be overcome in changing patterns of agricultural operation. The technological difficulties, however, even though numerous, are the most easily removed. The principal problems in the developing nations concern local attitudes, organizations, and infrastructures that are not properly geared to modern agricultural technology. Usually the public agricultural organization is highly bureaucratized; more often than not, it is weak, ill-supported, and poorly structured to achieve its purposes. At the same time, the efforts of developed nations to assist these countries have been hampered by conflicting views as to the seriousness of the world food problem and the approaches needed to solve it, by political and budgetary constraints, by bureaucratic inflexibility, and by frequent changes in goals.

Because of the low regard in which agricultural science has been held in all too many countries, those responsible for agricultural development often enjoy less professional esteem than those who dedicate their lives to fields regarded as more scholarly or academic. It is customary for representatives of agricultural institutions to receive lower salaries than those engaged in "less practical" pursuits. Budgets are usually inadequate, and frequently the money, manpower, materials, and other components essential for a successful agricultural industry are not available at the right time for the right purpose. It is now time for agrarian nations desiring economic and social progress to recognize agriculture as an important basic industry, whose welfare is essential to the national welfare, and to express this recognition by according agriculture a position of prominence and respect and by investng men, money, and materials in its personnel, programs, and institutions.

Agriculture, which clearly was undergoing evolutionary progress throughout the world until the period following World War II, has now entered a revolutionary phase in the developed nations. And, in a very few of the developing nations, revolutionary changes are occurring with certain crops in certain restricted regions. The

world clearly has the technical capability to extend the revolution
to all crops and domesticated animals in virtually all areas. However, the likelihood of a tremendous increase in numbers of people
in the decades ahead, particularly in areas of lowest agricultural
productivity, constitutes a challenge of momentous proportions.
Until major populations are stabilized, and until most nations
seriously devote attention and resources to accelerated agricultural
production, the future welfare of mankind must remain in doubt.

But we believe that the challenge can be met. Man has it within
his power to make this "the age of beneficent agricultural revolution," and we believe that he will do it. He must also adjust his
numbers to his means of subsistence, and we have faith that he will
do that too—and by intelligent means.

Suggested Further Reading

Borlaug, Norman, "Wheat, Rust, and People," *Phytopathology,* 55 (1965),
1088–98.

Brown, Lester R., *Man, Land and Food: Looking Ahead at World Food
Needs,* Foreign Agricultural Economic Report No. 11. Washington:
U.S. Dept. of Agriculture, Economic Research Service, 1963.

——, *Increasing World Food Output: Problems and Prospects,* Foreign
Agricultural Economic Report No. 25. Washington: U.S. Dept. of Agriculture, Economic Research Service, 1965.

——, "The Agricultural Revolution in Asia," *Foreign Affairs,* 46:4
(July 1968), 688–98.

Harrar, J. G., "Bread and Peace," Occasional Paper. New York: The
Rockefeller Foundation, 1963.

——, "Principles for Progress in World Agriculture" (Address given
before the National Agricultural Chemicals Assoc., White Sulphur
Springs, West Virginia, September 8, 1966). New York: The Rockefeller
Foundation, 1966.

——, *Strategy Toward the Conquest of Hunger,* selected papers. New
York: The Rockefeller Foundation, 1967.

Johnson, D. Gale, *The Struggle Against World Hunger,* Headline Series
No. 184. New York: Foreign Policy Association, August 1967.

Mosher, A. T., *Getting Agriculture Moving: Essentials for Development and Modernization.* New York: Frederick A. Praeger, Inc., for the Agricultural Development Council, 1966.

The Rockefeller Foundation, *Progress Report on the Program in the Agricultural Sciences,* 1965–66.

———, *Strategy for the Conquest of Hunger, Proceedings of a Symposium,* held at Rockefeller University, April 1 and 2, 1968.

Schultz, Theodore W., *Transforming Traditional Agriculture.* New Haven, Conn.: Yale University Press, 1964.

———, "What Ails World Agriculture," *Bulletin of Atomic Scientists,* January 1968, pp. 28–35.

Stakman, E. C., Richard Bradfield, and Paul C. Mangelsdorf, *Campaigns Against Hunger.* Cambridge, Mass.: The Belknap Press of Harvard University Press, 1967.

Wortman, Sterling, "Making Agronomy Serve Developing Countries," in *Challenge to Agronomy for the Future,* Special Publication No. 10, American Society of Agronomy, 1967.

———, "Rice Research: A Race Against Time," *International Rice Comm. Newsletter* No. 13 (1964), pp. 1–14.

U.S. Science Advisory Committee of the President, *The World Food Problem,* a report. Washington: Govt. Printing Office, 1967.

David E. Bell, Lowell S. Hardin,
and F. F. Hill

4

Hope for the Hungry:
Fulfillment or Frustration?

This chapter addresses the question, what should the United
States do—through public and private means—to meet the problems and opportunities outlined above. In the light of the situation
with respect to population growth and food supply, what are the
requirements for assistance to the less-developed countries? What
part should the United States play in providing that assistance?
What is the likelihood that the needed United States resources will
be made available? What are the likely consequences of U.S. action
—or inaction?

DAVID E. BELL *is Vice President for International Affairs, and* LOWELL S.
HARDIN *and* FORREST F. HILL *are program advisors for agriculture at The
Ford Foundation. Mr. Bell has been Director of the Bureau of the Budget
and Administrator of AID, has lectured in economics at Harvard, and has
served as advisor to the planning board of the government of Pakistan.
Dr. Hardin taught agricultural economics at Cornell and Purdue Uni-
versities for many years. Dr. Hill, former Vice President of The Ford
Foundation, is Chairman of the Board of Directors of the International
Rice Research Institute.*

Limiting Population Growth

Dr. Notestein's chapter provides a forceful statement of the outlook for population growth. If birth control practices are energetically fostered, particularly in the less-developed regions, the
world's population, which was about 3 billion in 1960, is likely by
the end of the century to total between 5.5 and 6 billion. In the
absence of strong birth control measures the population would
likely be one billion larger. The conclusion is plain: the first requirement for dealing effectively with world hunger is to take
measures to limit population growth.

A few years ago, the primary obstacle to effective programs for
dealing with rapid population growth was the absence of favorable national policies and programs. That obstacle has been largely
overcome. Some 25 countries have now adopted official policies
encouraging family planning. Two events of 1967 symbolize the
change. In April, 1967, the International Planned Parenthood
Federation held its International Conference for the first time in
Latin America, at Santiago, and the opening session was addressed
by the President of Chile, Eduardo Frei. And in December, a dec-
laration underlining the importance of the population problem
and urging national and international action to deal with it was
presented to U Thant by 30 heads of government including the
Presidents or Prime Ministers of Colombia, India, the United
States, and Yugoslavia. Population policies in many countries including our own are still evolving and will change greatly in the
years ahead. But the major bridge has been crossed in most cases,
and despite occasional setbacks such as the Pope's statement in
July, 1968, that only the rhythm method of regulating fertility is
acceptable to the Roman Catholic Church, it is clear that the attitudes of governmental and private leaders around the world are
increasingly positive toward action to deal with the population
problem.

FIRST PRIORITY: RESEARCH

Today, the principal obstacle to effective population programs is inadequate contraceptive technology. A considerable variety of techniques is available, of which the newest and perhaps most widely used are the intrauterine devices (IUDs) and the anti-ovulation pills. All present techniques have significant defects for use in developing countries. The IUDs, for example, require many carefully trained people to supervise insertions, and about 50 per cent of women discontinue their use after two years. The anti-ovulation pills in their present form require continuous and sophisticated use under medical supervision, and half of pill users in developing countries discontinue their use in only one year. Troublesome side effects limit the acceptability of both methods for some women, and longer experience with both is identifying more clearly the associated medical risks they entail.

The disadvantages of current techniques have not, of course, prevented the establishment of public or private family planning programs. Indeed, the advent of the IUD greatly aided the most effective large scale programs now in existence, those in Taiwan and Korea. Nevertheless, the disadvantages of current technology sharply limit the accomplishments of present programs and make their administration complex and difficult. In particular, because they require so many highly trained persons, programs based on current techniques have difficulty in making a major impact in rural areas.

Consequently the most important requirement for more effective family planning in less-developed countries is simpler and cheaper means for preventing conception, which in turn requires substantially greater research in the field of reproductive biology. This research will have to be conducted for the most part, over the next decade, in the laboratories and hospitals of more advanced countries where the necessary scientists and scientific resources are to be found. Increasingly, however, research of an international standard of quality is being carried on in less-developed countries. This is true, for example, at certain research centers in Brazil, India, and Mexico.

Neither in the advanced nor the developing countries is a sufficiently large-scale attack being launched on this problem to explore adequately all the promising lines of research that are now in sight. Substantially larger funds are needed not only to support the researchers now in the field but to attract more talent. At a rough guess, perhaps $25–30 million worth of high quality research relevant to fertility control is now being done per year. Our colleagues, Drs. Anna L. Southam and Oscar Harkavy, estimate that five or six times this sum would be necessary for an optimum research effort which could be achieved after a build-up of several years.[1]

SUPPORT FOR ACTION PROGRAMS

The second priority need is to support the development of action programs using the best techniques available. The evidence is clear that determined effort and able management have enabled the family planning programs in Taiwan, Korea, Singapore, and Hong Kong to have a measurable impact in reducing birth rates. (The calculations are complex, since they involve an attempt to isolate the influence of organized family planning programs from the increased use of birth control measures that are expected concomitants of the spread of education, the gradual rise in incomes, and other indices of modernization. But the demographers are now satisfied that family planning programs are having a significant effect in those countries.)[2]

Foreign assistance can be of considerable help in several ways. Most important is to provide opportunities for health personnel, economists, sociologists, demographers, and other relevant professionals in each developing country to become thoroughly competent in the population field. Population problems and family planning involve questions of extraordinary sensitivity and the public leaders in any country must make decisions of great delicacy. Each country must decide, for example, whether to permit the use of new contraceptive techniques and, if so, under what standards of safety.

[1] See "Resources for Research in Reproductive Biology," in Harkavy, *et al.*, *Implementing DHEW Policy on Family Planning and Population*, Department of Health, Education, and Welfare, September, 1967.
[2] See, for example, "Korea and Taiwan: The Record for 1967," *Studies in Family Planning*, No. 29, Population Council, April, 1968.

Such decisions—whether they involve medical, social science, or moral judgments—should be based on the advice of leading professional experts in each country, and training and institutional support for such experts is a most important type of technical assistance.

In addition, technical advice and training, and in some cases equipment and supplies, can be of assistance to the agencies, public or private or both, which are undertaking to make family planning information and supplies widely available in developing countries. A great deal of experimentation on the best means for providing family planning services is now underway, and there is much debate over such questions as whether family planning services should be provided separately or only as part of a broader system of maternal and child health care, whether the head of the national family planning organization should or should not report to the director-general of health, and how far it will be efficient to rely on commercial distribution of contraceptives. Far too little experience is available as yet to permit dogmatism on such questions, and indeed the likelihood is that differences in circumstances will require different solutions in different countries. Outside advisers can offer no blueprints, but can be helpful in identifying alternative solutions to questions of policy and administration, and in establishing systems of recruitment and training of family planning personnel, reporting and evaluation of program effectiveness, etc.

IS VOLUNTARISM ENOUGH?

In addition to these two requirements for assistance—support for research and for action programs—a third is beginning to appear. Until now, the general assumption on which family planning programs have been based is that most people in most countries would like to control the number and spacing of their children. Knowledge, attitude, and practice (KAP) studies wherever they are conducted support this assumption.[3] But there is also a real ques-

---

[3] See "Fertility Studies: Knowledge, Attitude, and Practice," *Studies in Family Planning*, No. 7, Population Council, June, 1965.

tion, most strongly stated perhaps by Professor Kingsley Davis,[4] whether the individual decisions of separate families will result in an optimal rate of population growth for each country and for the world. Davis makes the assumption that only a zero rate of population growth is acceptable in the long run, which is a debatable assumption. But his basic question—whether the working of individual motivation will yield socially desirable results—is clearly valid.

This raises a wide variety of issues of a practical and theoretical nature. Are there measures of public policy in such fields as taxation, family allowances, and education which could influence decisions on family size in one direction or another? How far could a country go along the spectrum of influence from verbal persuasion through economic incentives without reaching the area of coercion, which many people reject on moral grounds? Or is it any longer appropriate with the possibility of a population crisis confronting the world to shrink from some degree of coercion?

These are among the questions which many countries will confront in the years ahead. They will require for their sensible solution much careful research and thoughtful analysis, involving not only medical and social scientists but philosophers and moralists. Some of the research and analysis can be—indeed will need to be—conducted in the advanced countries which face these questions with respect to their own people. More of it will need to be conducted in the developing countries, and this offers a fruitful field for collaborative research among scholars around the world.

NEED FOR MORE ASSISTANCE

All this adds up to the possibility of a strong potential contribution to population programs in the developing countries through assistance from the advanced countries. There is little relevant experience in a direct sense: none of the advanced countries has so far conducted a national family planning program. But there is relevant experience with smaller scale programs. And more im-

[4] "Population Policy: Will Current Programs Succeed?" *Science*, Nov. 10, 1967.

portant, there are resources for scientific research and for management advice and training, as well as material resources, which can be brought to bear.

In fact, the availability of assistance in the population field has been rising very rapidly in recent years. In the middle and late fifties, the private foundations were just beginning to move on from the support of demographic research and training to the support of research in reproductive biology and of action programs in developing countries. In the early sixties, the Agency for International Development was taking its first cautious steps toward assisting family planning, as were the National Institutes of Health toward research in this field. Some other national aid programs, notably that of Sweden, were also beginning to be active in family planning. The International Planned Parenthood Federation was beginning to seek larger funds and broader coverage. The U.N. and its specialized agencies have moved even more recently and are just beginning to undertake programs directed toward fertility control.

Many governments in both advanced and developing countries have changed their views in this field—and changed with a speed exemplified by President Eisenhower, who in the late 1950's barred any U.S. Government support for family planning, but less than ten years later was advocating the opposite as Honorary Co-Chairman, along with President Truman, of Planned Parenthood/World Population. Private interest has also mushroomed. So far, however, the resources made available for assistance are only a fraction of what will be needed. Within a few years, up to $150 million for research and perhaps an equal amount for other types of help could be well used each year. The U.S. Government is the only likely source for perhaps two-thirds of these funds—against which at present it is budgeting $10 to $15 million for research in reproductive biology and $30 to $35 million for assistance to family planning programs in developing countries. The very slow rise in NIH funds devoted to research in reproductive biology is cause for special concern, since it means that the highest priority requirement in the field at the present time—and a requirement the United States is especially well qualified to meet—is being inadequately financed.

At the present time, therefore, it is not possible to see more than the outlines of a possible pattern of satisfactory financing and management for assistance in this field. The private foundations have supported much of the pioneering work and can be expected to continue to finance some of the more novel and experimental work—but cannot provide more than a small part of the total funds needed. Business financing could perhaps be expected to contribute more than it has so far, both in supporting research and through commercial distribution of contraceptives. Most of the funds needed for research and assistance, however, must surely come from governments, both through bilateral aid programs and—if the U.N. develops effective programs in the future—through multilateral channels.

It is particularly to be hoped that the U.N. will develop a strong program in the population field, because in this sensitive area politically neutral, internationally-based advice and assistance could have obvious advantages. It will not be easy for the U.N. to mount a comprehensive program, however, because of the fragmented nature of its organization—with the World Health Organization responsible for technical assistance in health programs but having no funds for equipment, which however can be provided by the U.N. Children's Fund (UNICEF), and with the Population Division of the U.N. Secretariat responsible for demographic work and for questions of population policy in relation to national development. Steps are now being undertaken to provide better coordinating arrangements. If these arrangements are successful, and if the U.N. becomes a strong and active leader in the population field, it would be appropriate for advanced countries to channel an increasing share of their assistance to population programs through that organization.

Providing Food Supplies

Dr. Notestein has also given us a forceful statement of the growing requirements for food supplies. The world which provided inadequate diets for a large proportion of its 3 billion people in 1960 faces the problem of feeding about twice that number by the year 2000 even if strenuous efforts are made to reduce birth rates.

The problem is made more difficult by the fact that most of the increase in population will come in the less-developed regions. Moreover, demands for food in less-developed countries will rise faster than population growth rates as per capita incomes rise and people seek to improve their levels of nutrition.

All this adds up to the need for rates of increase in agricultural production in developing countries that are very high by historical standards. As Dr. Paarlberg points out in his chapter, the need is for rates of increase in grain production in developing countries on the order of 4 per cent per year—which would be nearly double their historic rates, and, incidentally, would be substantially higher rates than the United States has had over recent decades.

Nevertheless, this does not appear to be an impossible task. Something like a technological breakthrough seems to be occurring in food production—though the process is still at so early a stage that one should beware of over-confidence.[5] In substantial areas of India, Pakistan, the Philippines, and a number of other developing countries, new varieties of wheat, of rice, and of other food grains, which are capable of converting large amounts of fertilizer into heavy grain yields, are producing two and three times as much grain per acre as the varieties they are replacing. In the case of rice, some of the new heavier-yielding varieties also ripen in a shorter time, allowing two and in some cases three crops per year to be grown where one or two were grown before.

These gains are beginning to show up in national output figures. They have played a part in the large 1967–68 Indian harvest of between 95 and 100 million tons of food grains. And they underlie the dramatic fact that the Philippines in 1968 moved into a substantial rice export position for the first time since 1900.

Much more is involved in such results, of course, than new vari-

[5] For a good summary, see Lester R. Brown, "The Agricultural Revolution in Asia," *Foreign Affairs*, July, 1968.

eties alone. A complete technology is required: new varieties plus improved sowing and cultivation practices plus applications of fertilizer and water plus protection measures against plant diseases and pests plus improved harvesting, drying, threshing, and storage methods. Any or all of these elements may change radically as a result of the new varieties. For example, the new third crop of rice in Thanjavur District in southern India matures in the rainy season, requiring the introduction of wholly new mechanical drying methods in place of the older sun-drying system. For another example, the preparation of the land between crops in Ludhiana District in northern India requires operations of such speed and precision as to give great advantage to tractor over bullock power, and the rural nights in the Punjab are beginning to be lighted—as in Iowa—by the headlamps of tractors working through the dark hours.

The geographic reach of the new technology should not be exaggerated. For maximum increases in yields, favorable conditions are required—particularly adequate water supplies—which means at least for the present that only modest increases in yields can be expected on millions of cultivated areas without sufficient rainfall or irrigation to permit heavy fertilization. Improved varieties and methods have not yet been developed, moreover, for some important crops and types of soils. The new technology will be adopted only where economic policies—particularly policies relating to prices—are such as to provide sufficient incentives to farmers. And there must be enough of the necessary production supplies (fertilizer, pesticides, etc.) and trained manpower (the relatively small numbers of specialists in agronomy, plant protection, etc., and the larger numbers of extension agents or their equivalent).

Putting these same conditions in positive form, however, permits us to say that in those areas of the less-developed countries where conditions are favorable—and this means many millions of acres— a combination of newly developed production technology, proper economic policies, and sufficient production supplies and trained agricultural manpower can be counted on to achieve radical increases in the output of principal food crops. Such increases are now occurring in many places in the developing countries, and are the evidence that we may be witnessing an historic breakthrough in food production in those countries.

The sound policy line for the less-developed countries, therefore, is to follow up all elements of the production breakthrough with maximum energy. It will not be easy to provide the needed supplies and manpower, to conduct the adaptive research required to keep a flow of newer varieties in the pipeline as earlier ones succumb to pests and diseases, to develop better systems of water control and management (including drainage), and to maintain incentives as prices respond to larger production. New problems will arrive with greater output—such as the need for much larger storage and transport capacity. And the political effects will be large —including the painful strains on the social and political fabric as agricultural areas with favorable land and water conditions begin to jump ahead in output and income in contrast to areas with less favorable conditions. But if the necessary talent and resources are applied, there seems to be a real chance that food production can be increased rapidly enough to keep up with demand while effective population measures are being developed.

BREAKTHROUGHS REQUIRE AID

As is the case with any aspect of development, the bulk of the resources and the effort required must come from the developing countries themselves. But certain crucial resources are required that cannot be found in those countries or purchased by them in their present economic circumstances. For example, many (though by no means all) of the new crop varieties now showing good results were developed at the international research centers on wheat, corn, and rice which have been established by the Rockefeller and Ford foundations. And much of the fertilizer necessary to produce the bumper 1967–68 crop of food grains in India was financed by the United States Agency for International Development.

If the agricultural breakthrough is to proceed, therefore, substantial foreign assistance—both technical and financial—will be needed for some years to come. The nature and dimensions of those assistance requirements must be clearly understood if correct policies are to be followed.

RESEARCH AND DEVELOPMENT

To raise agricultural production rapidly and continuously in developing countries requires first of all a system of technological research and development. It has been proven over and over again that the agricultural technology that is successful in the United States or other advanced countries cannot be transferred without adaptation. The varieties of seeds and methods of cultivation that produce bumper crops in the Midwest will not do so in India or Brazil. This should not surprise us. It has taken decades of scientific work in our land-grant universities and of trial and error by our farmers to find the particular adaptations and combinations that work best in the various parts of the United States. Exactly the same effort is required—on an accelerated time table—in the less-developed countries.

Nor is this task something that can be done once and forgotten. Producing higher-yielding varieties of seeds, for example, is a never-ending task, because new scientific discoveries are continually opening up new opportunities, and because pests and diseases are continually adapting their attack and a new variety that is stout and strong when introduced is likely to have to be replaced within a few years.

To build a technological research and development system for agriculture in the less-developed countries is a difficult task. To achieve it will require a substantial and long-continued effort, primarily by way of technical cooperation and financial assistance directed to the slow process of building scientific and technological competence. This is not just a process of teaching young scientists from the developing countries. Many young scientists need to be trained, but there are already a substantial number of high competence. A Mexican scientist, for example, is the principal scientific adviser to the Government of West Pakistan in introducing the new short-strawed wheats in that country; an Indian scientist is Associate Director of the International Rice Research Institute in the Philippines.

A more difficult task than the training of young scientists is the complex and intricate process by which scientific institutions in less-developed countries are raised in competence and effectively harnessed to the practical development problems of their countries. To do this effectively will require cooperative arrangements among national institutions in the developing countries, regional centers such as IRRI, and research centers in advanced countries.

OTHER INSTITUTIONS

Institutions for technological research and development are not enough in themselves to support a strongly growing agriculture. Educational institutions must be shaped—not only colleges to produce trained agricultural specialists but also primary and secondary schools in rural communities. Institutions—mostly governmental—to provide advice and services to farmers must be improved. Agricultural credit institutions must be expanded since the financial requirements for a productive and expanding agriculture will rise very sharply. Outside assistance both of a technical and capital nature can be of great help toward many of these objectives.

GREATER SUPPLY LINES NEEDED

The new agricultural technology creates skyrocketing demands for agricultural supplies and equipment. For example, it is expected that farmers' use of fertilizer in India will rise more than six-fold in seven years—from 600,000 tons in 1963–64 to 4 million tons in 1970–71.

To meet these demands in the short run requires a radical increase in imports. The most spectacular example is India, which expects to require imports of fertilizer costing on the order of $300 million per year for each of the next several years while domestic plants are under construction—and much of this must be financed by outside assistance.

The longer run answer of course is to expand domestic manufacturing capacity to the extent that this can be done economically. And in any event the channels for distribution and supply of agricultural equipment and supplies must be greatly enlarged. In many countries this is a difficult task, since traditional supply and distribution systems both governmental and non-governmental will need radical change.

In many cases, experience is demonstrating that private business organizations can play an effective role in meeting these needs. To cite India again, there has been a steady shift in opinion in that country, moving from an insistence on government ownership of all fertilizer plants to an increasingly wide participation by private business both Indian and foreign in the fertilizer industry. There has been a parallel shift from a cooperatives-only distribution policy toward an open policy permitting private companies to establish direct distribution systems to the extent they may wish to do so.

Foreign knowledge and capital can be of very great help in this area, and private business organizations in the advanced countries can play an especially valuable role where they are given an opportunity to do so. Organizations like the new Agribusiness Council in the United States can be of great help in identifying opportunities for business activity and obstacles—of government policy or otherwise—to their fulfillment.

POLICIES FOR AGRICULTURAL GROWTH

The process of rapid agricultural growth cannot occur unless there are favorable national policies. The most conspicuous—and probably the most important—illustration is the policy regarding price incentives. Farmers everywhere are canny in calculating their own interests, and will respond to new technical possibilities only if the economic returns are sufficient to cover the costs and reward the risks of innovation. To establish and maintain incentive prices for agricultural products must therefore be a central objective of policy in developing countries.

Other policy questions are also of high importance, including the crucial issues of what priority should be given agriculture within the overall national development program; what reliance should be placed on the private sector in matters of manufacturing and supply of agricultural inputs (as well as matters of storage, transport, and processing of agricultural outputs); how agriculture is to be taxed; how land tenure problems are to be resolved; and how scarce budget resources should be allocated among the many elements of an integrated program for agricultural growth.

Outside assistance can help in these policy areas by providing training, assistance in analysis, and advice where needed to policy-makers and their staffs, and by supporting research to provide a stronger basis for policy-making. These are types of assistance which are delicate to handle, because they necessarily involve sensitive issues. But they are also types of assistance which if handled successfully, can have a very large impact on food production.

NOT BY AGRICULTURE ALONE

Finally, agriculture cannot develop by itself. There is no such thing as an effective program for agricultural development except as part of a broader program for national development. By the same token, there is no such thing as an effective program of external assistance to agricultural growth except as part of a broader program of assistance to general economic growth.

These are very important points, with much practical significance. They rest on the plain fact that if agricultural production is to grow in developing countries, changes must occur far beyond the reaches of the agricultural sector. If increased agricultural output is to be sold, internal markets must grow, based on rising urban and industrial incomes. Transportation, storage, and marketing must be enlarged and improved. Fertilizers, insecticides and machinery must be manufactured or imported and in either case distributed. Financial and credit facilities must be expanded. Educational and research systems must be developed.

Similarly, the growth of incomes and purchasing power in the agricultural sector is essential to broader national economic growth. What is required is a mutually-supporting process, involving simultaneous advances in both agriculture and industry, with the nature and dimensions of the advance in each sector being adapted to the resources, markets, and other conditions of the country in question.

A sensible program of foreign assistance to agricultural growth in developing countries must include, therefore, in addition to measures aimed directly at the agricultural sector, support for the general growth of the economy. Only as the general economy is strengthened can agriculture grow.

THE QUESTION OF QUANTITY

For reasons just outlined, the question of how much aid is required to achieve rapid increases in agricultural production in less-developed countries necessarily involves the broader question: how much aid is required to achieve general economic growth, including rapid progress in agriculture. It is not easy to make reliable estimates; the subject is inherently complex and any conclusions depend heavily on judgment factors. Nevertheless, in recent years, some progress has been made in estimating aid requirements.

Such estimates normally rest on the concept that from the viewpoint of both aid-receiver and aid-giver it is important to plan assistance in such a way that it will lead to a self-sustaining process of further growth. Aid should be conceived of, that is to say, as an investment process, which results in permanent gains in the productive capacity of the developing countries, and is intended to bring about an economic growth process sustained not by aid but by normal commercial trade and capital movements. From this point of view, there is no difference in principle between aid in the form of food and aid in the form of capital equipment or raw materials or technical services. The question in each case is whether the aid in question is necessary to support a development program that will achieve self-sustaining growth. (This concept of the proper nature of an aid program includes, of course, the possibility of providing food aid to meet an emergency such as crop failure, but would require—as the United States has recently been doing—that the receiving country organize a program for permanent improvement and not simply one for temporary relief, in order to qualify for food aid.)

A concept of aid as investment provides a reasonably clear basis for judgment on how much aid is required for particular countries at any given time. The calculation starts with the development program that is necessary for a country to move toward self-sustaining growth at the maximum feasible rate (note that what is called for is not a simple application of econometric formulas, but a hardheaded, practical judgment of what can actually be accomplished, given sensible policies and maximum effort). Then estimates can be made of how much of the resources needed from abroad to support the development program can be financed through the country's own foreign exchange earnings and through foreign private investment. The difference represents what is needed through aid —although this conventional terminology blurs the fact that some substantial share (perhaps one-fifth) of what is usually termed "aid" is in fact borrowing at commercial rates, and that different countries can afford different mixes of borrowing at commercial and at subsidized rates.

Using the conventional terminology, the flow of aid from advanced to developing countries has been around $6.5 billion per year (net of repayments on previous aid loans). The flow of private investment has fluctuated roughly between $2.5 and $3.5 billion.[6] According to IBRD estimates, as stated by the former President of the Bank, George Woods, in a number of speeches, perhaps $3 to $4 billion of additional capital investment per year (most of which would have to be aid, not private investment) would be needed to enable developing countries to make maximum progress toward self-sustaining growth—and by the same token, to end the need for aid at the earliest feasible time. Such an estimate is in a sense a maximum figure. It assumes that all developing countries would be prepared to commit themselves to strong and effective development programs, thus justifying full-scale external assistance. This would surely not be true; one must anticipate always some ineffective governments in aid-receiving countries. Nevertheless it is clear that more aid than is currently being made available could be well

[6] These figures, based on data through calendar year 1966, are drawn from the report of Willard Thorp, Chairman of the Development Assistance Committee, OECD, entitled *Development Assistance Efforts and Policies, 1967 Review*, Paris, September 1967. Preliminary figures for calendar year 1967 show an encouraging rise—based almost entirely on increases from countries other than the United States—to $7.5 billion of aid plus $4 billion of private investment.

used by developing countries, and would significantly speed the day when they will have achieved self-sustaining growth.

In summary, it may be useful to think of the requirements for aid to achieve self-sustaining growth, including rapid agricultural growth, as of the order of $8–10 billion per year for the next few years. This would be in addition to private foreign investment which over this period can be expected to grow from its recent level but only slowly. There will be a tendency for aid requirements to rise in some developing countries which are gaining competence and establishing better development policies; this will be offset to some extent by the decline in requirements in countries—such as Korea and Turkey—which are well along toward a self-sustaining growth process and increasingly able to meet their needs for external financing on a commercial basis.

Implications for U.S. Policy

How should the United States respond to the requirements for assistance that have been outlined in the preceding pages? Assuming for the moment that our national priorities give a high place to helping meet the world's food and population problems—a point that will be discussed below—an efficient program for doing so might include the following elements:

1. Expanded support for research in some important fields, especially reproductive biology and contraceptive technology. Such research should be supported directly in U.S. institutions (notably through NIH), as well as through the development and use of research capacity abroad. Most of the funds for this will need to come from the U.S. Government, although some can come from foundations, drug companies, and other private sources.

2. Expanded U.S. private activity in developing countries— notably private business investment (including the training and community support activities common in enlightened modern business policy); private cooperation in educational and cultural fields (including exchanges of students and faculty, cooperative research, etc.); the work of private foundations (including sup-

port for research and technical assistance); and the activities of U.S. voluntary agencies, religious and secular (including support for educational, medical, agricultural and industrial activities). U.S. private business investment in developing countries has averaged about $1 billion per year in recent years, although there is naturally considerable fluctuation from year to year; a large share of the total in most years has been for petroleum.

3. Expanded public support for private activity. A steadily wider range of activities has been developed in recent years, mostly through the Agency for International Development, to support U.S. private business investment in developing countries and other types of private action which contribute to development. Among the activities which have been most successful are: investment guarantees of various types, of which the largest in volume (now about $5 billion) is insurance against the loss of business investment owing to expropriation, war damage, or inconvertibility of currency; support for the International Executive Service Corps, a privately organized service of technical assistance by American businessmen to businessmen in developing countries; and paying transportation costs for gifts of tools, food, books, and other useful items by U.S. voluntary organizations such as CARE and many others. It should be possible with experience steadily to improve and expand the variety of types of support for private developmental action at relatively low cost to the Federal budget.

4. Expanded U.S. Government assistance for development— both technical assistance and capital assistance—through both multilateral and bilateral channels, on terms that can be varied to fit the balance of payments circumstances of different aid-receiving countries. Assuming there were an internationally-agreed effort by the advanced countries to meet the assistance requirements outlined above, the U.S. Government share might appropriately be 50–60 per cent of the total, since the U.S. GNP is roughly 50–60 per cent of the total GNP of the advanced countries. If the total requirement for effective aid were $8–10 billion per year for the next several years, as suggested by Mr.

Woods' statements, the U.S. share would be of the order of $4.5–6 billion. This $4.5–6 billion might consist of $300–500 million of technical assistance (bilateral and multilateral); $1–1.5 billion of food aid; $1–2 billion of contributions in various forms to the capital of the international banks (some of which would be raised on the money market rather than provided in the Federal budget); and $1.5–2.5 billion of bilateral capital assistance. (In comparable terms, the current total is of the order of $3.5–4 billion.)

5. Policies in the fields of international trade and monetary arrangements which give special support to the economic growth of developing countries. Recent illustrations of such policies include the agreement in principle which was reached at the Second United Nations Conference on Trade and Development, in New Delhi, that general tariff preferences should be given by the advanced countries to manufactured products from the developing countries, on some sort of arrangement which would scale the preferences gradually down to zero as the manufacturing industries in question achieve maturity and competitive strength. Another illustration of such a policy is the recent suggestion made with respect to the new Special Drawing Rights from the IMF, that a share of any Rights which are issued be made available for the use of the developing countries.

All these elements of a policy to support the growth of developing countries, giving top priority to food and population problems, would be sound and valuable in terms of the requirements of those countries. Together they might cost the United States between ½ and 1 per cent of GNP. If coupled with strong development programs on the part of the developing countries themselves, and matching aid from other advanced countries, this U.S. policy could have very important effects in the developing countries in a period, say, of five to ten years.

And yet major elements of this policy are under strong attack in the U.S. Congress, and among important elements of U.S. public opinion—particularly the elements involving U.S. Government assistance. Questions are raised based on a number of different grounds.

MAJOR QUESTIONS ABOUT FOREIGN AID

Can aid do any good?—There are, first, several questions about the effectiveness of foreign assistance. Perhaps the most central is whether external aid can help significantly. Are not the elements of apathy, ignorance, archaic social structures, and other characteristics of developing countries so disabling that only very slow gains can be made, and these induced not by foreign help but by domestic forces in the less-developed countries? There is by now strong evidence to the contrary. Numerous cases can be cited which show how foreign assistance, properly used in conjunction with domestic resources, by good local leadership in a strong development program, have in fact brought about rapid development which could not have been achieved without such foreign aid. In a recent book[7] Dean Neil H. Jacoby of the University of California (Los Angeles) describes one such situation, in which the process of self-sustaining growth has been established and foreign aid brought to a successful conclusion. Dr. Mason's study, *Economic Development in India and Pakistan*,[8] describes the surprisingly rapid progress in Pakistan resulting from sound policies plus substantial economic aid. Pakistan has not yet reached a position of self-sustaining growth but has been making good headway in that direction.

Far from feeling that the situation in less-developed countries is hopeless, development economists are increasingly confident that they can design, in nearly every case, a program combining domestic policies and resources plus external aid which can ensure substantial progress. The obstacles are indeed severe, and strong and intelligent leadership in the developing countries is necessary to overcome them —but external assistance is also a crucial ingredient to achieve rapid

[7] Neil H. Jacoby, *U.S. Aid to Taiwan* (New York: Frederick A. Praeger, Inc., 1966).

[8] Edward S. Mason, *Economic Development in India and Pakistan*, Harvard University Center for International Affairs, Occasional Paper Number 13, September 1966.

economic and social change, except in the cases of the few developing countries blessed by ample foreign exchange resources (resulting usually from petroleum exports).

To avoid any misunderstanding, it should be noted that no assertion is being made that the achievement of self-sustaining growth will usher in the millennium in developing countries. Taiwan reached this stage at a per capita income level of less than $200. Many and serious problems confront the Taiwanese; the key point is that their economy is now strong enough and growing fast enough (over 7 per cent per year) so that they can deal successfully with their own problems in the future by relying on normal commercial trade and capital markets. This condition appears to be attainable in many more developing countries over the next decade or two. Whether it will in fact be attained will depend crucially on the quality of local leadership and the volume of external aid.

Why can't private enterprise do the job?—A second question that is often raised is why private enterprise can't do the development job. The growth of the U.S. economy, it is asserted, was accomplished with substantial foreign investment but no foreign aid. Why can't today's developing countries do the same?

We can indeed ask developing countries to follow stringent policies to do the most they can for themselves—to mobilize resources through taxation, to accept reasonable repayment burdens for resources obtained from abroad, to limit consumption and to direct a maximum share of resources to productive investment. There is some encouraging evidence that the need for such policies is increasingly widely understood—see for example the recent rapid increases in tax collections in a number of Latin American countries as a result of firmer enforcement of the tax laws against upper income groups.

But strong development policies will yield different results in countries with different resource endowments. It was mentioned above that a few countries are fortunate enough to have ample foreign exchange earnings; such countries (Saudi Arabia, for example, or Libya) can indeed be expected to obtain the physical goods they need on ordinary commercial terms (by purchase or borrowing).

They may even be expected to pay for the technical advice, training, and other types of technical assistance they need, although this may raise special difficulties such as the political problems incident to having to pay a U.S. or European expert or teacher several times as much as an equally well qualified national.

Most countries are not so fortunate. Their foreign exchange earnings fall far short of covering their minimum needs for imports of capital goods and raw materials. In such circumstances, foreign investors are not easily attracted; they have legitimate worries about whether future foreign exchange receipts of the developing country concerned will permit the transfer of interest, amortization, and earnings on their investments. Indeed one way of formulating the problem of establishing a self-sustaining development process in any country is to say that it requires an economy growing fast enough, and with a strong enough balance of payments (present and prospective) so that it can reasonably expect to obtain the foreign capital it requires through commercial borrowing and private foreign investment. To reach that position—to get from here to there—will in most cases require considerable foreign assistance, a point that is well understood by leading American businessmen concerned with the developing countries.[9]

The comparison with the United States in the nineteenth century is thoroughly misleading. North America was, comparatively, a vast empty storehouse of natural resources waiting to be tapped, highly attractive to outside capital—almost the opposite of countries like India or Pakistan today which are heavily populated and already pressing against the margins of their modest endowments of natural resources. The inevitable conclusion is that while private investment can do part of the job, and every effort should be made in developing and advanced countries to enlarge its contribution, a combination of publicly-supported foreign assistance and of private business investment is necessary to get the job of development done.

Should we switch from bilateral to multilateral assistance?—Another question often raised about the effectiveness of U.S. assistance

[9] Cf. for example David Rockefeller, "The Case for Foreign Aid," Address at Council on Foreign Relations, Chicago, April 18, 1967.

is whether bilateral aid should not be eliminated in favor of multi-lateral aid?

There are important potential advantages to multilateral aid, principally the relatively greater opportunity for a multilateral aid donor to base judgments on technical rather than political grounds. It should be noted that these advantages do not accrue automatically and there are unfortunately examples of multilateral agencies which administer aid weakly. But given equal managerial competence and appropriate organizational arrangements, the advantages of the multilateral form are real.

For this reason, United States policy for the past decade has been strongly to promote multilateral forms of assistance to the limit of the willingness of other advanced countries to share in their financing. Multilateral aid by definition requires multilateral financing, and thus far some of the other advanced countries have been less willing than has the United States to raise their contributions. For example, in the recent round of negotiations over enlarging the resources of the International Development Association, it was finally possible only to obtain agreement among donors to raise the annual total from $250 million per year to $400 million per year (in this case the U.S. share of the total is 40 per cent), although it is generally agreed that the World Bank (which administers IDA) is a highly effective aid donor, and Mr. George Woods had originally asked for annual contributions to IDA totalling $1 billion.

The Bank's new president, Mr. Robert McNamara, can be expected to press vigorously to enlarge the flow of resources through international channels, and in his early months as president succeeded in raising significant funds for the Bank by selling Bank bonds in Germany, Kuwait, and elsewhere. Funds obtained by the Bank in this way, however, must be loaned by the Bank to developing countries at relatively high rates of interest; loans of this type do not meet the needs of the most difficult cases, such as India and Pakistan, which are already heavily burdened with interest costs. Further Bank lending to such countries is planned to be made primarily on the less stringent IDA terms—but this will be possible only with a more generous attitude on the part of the United States and other countries in making IDA funds available to the Bank.

It seems clear therefore as a practical matter that there are fairly severe limits to the degree to which assistance to the developing countries can be channelled through multilateral agencies. At the present time, only about 15–20 per cent of all aid flows through such agencies, and the proportion is not likely to rise dramatically over the next few years.

Against this somewhat discouraging prospect, however, must be set the fact that in recent years, new methods have been devised for obtaining many of the benefits of multilateral aid while retaining bilateral control of funds. Several different arrangements have been devised. Their common characteristics are that multilateral and bilateral aid donors act jointly, under the leadership of an international agency (as in the World Bank's consultative groups), in negotiating with an aid-receiving country concerning the amount and types of aid that are needed, and the self-help measures that the aid-receiving country commits itself to undertake as a condition of aid. Such arrangements have the advantage of permitting an international agency to take the lead in discussions of self-help measures and aid requirements while retaining with the various bilateral participants the flexibility and power of ultimate decision that seems to be required by aid-giving countries. There has been a very rapid growth of such arrangements; in recent years well over three-quarters of U.S. bilateral lending (administered by AID) has been managed within the framework of such multilateral arrangements.

Better methods for providing technical assistance?—One other question relating to the effectiveness of U.S. aid may be mentioned though it relates more to the views of technical experts than to those of Congress and the general public. This is the question whether a major gain in the effectiveness of U.S. technical assistance could be obtained by establishing a separate technical assistance organization —usually described as similar to the National Science Foundation— rather than combining technical and capital assistance in AID as has been the case since 1961.

There are strong arguments on both sides of this issue. The present arrangement, based on the concept of "country programming"—examining each country and determining the priorities appropriate to its needs—has the advantages of encouraging mutually supporting capital and technical assistance activities (one is less likely at least in theory to wind up with agricultural experiment stations without agricultural scientists, or vice versa) and of requiring the priority of each technical assistance project to be tested against standards of national development and not simply professional or sectoral standards. On the other hand, it has been suggested that a separate technical assistance agency could provide advantages of greater professionalism and continuity, although it would raise new problems of coordination. On balance, it would seem that the main improvements that are wanted would depend on Congressional authorization of longer-term projects and more freedom and flexibility to deal with organizations providing professional services; if these were given to AID there would be less reason to seek a separate technical assistance agency; if they were not given to a separate agency little would be gained from the change.

Can the U.S. afford foreign assistance?—Another group of questions about U.S. foreign aid relates not to effectiveness but to cost. Can we spare the resources for foreign assistance given the large competing demands on our budget? If our Federal budget can afford the cost, can our national balance of payments?

In one sense these questions are not difficult to answer. Federal resources of $4–6 billion per year devoted to foreign assistance would be well under one per cent of GNP, and well under ten per cent of what we spend each year on military defenses. If foreign assistance can be successful in ameliorating serious problems in the world and reducing the chances of future conflict, surely these would be small prices to pay. Such expenditures would have an extremely high benefit/cost ratio, and would not significantly interfere with our ability to meet other urgent problems such as education and urban redevelopment.

So far as the balance of payments is concerned, the United States has changed its policies in recent years so that with small exceptions assistance is provided in the form of goods and services and not in the form of freely convertible foreign exchange. When we provide

American food or tractors or fertilizer or technical advisers there is little if any adverse effect on the U.S. balance of payments. In total, less than ten per cent of aid outlays at present result in balance of payments costs—and again if aid serves important national interests, this would seem to be an acceptably low cost.

What's in it for us?—This brings us to what appears to be the central issue in the Congress at the present time—not the effectiveness nor the cost of assistance but the meaning and value to the United States of contributing to the solution of these problems. Put bluntly, the question is, why should the U.S. care? What interests of ours are deeply enough engaged to impel us to provide assistance? What, that is to say, is the foreign policy justification for spending money to help the less-developed countries?

The question is especially pertinent at the present time when the general outlines of U.S. foreign policy over the past twenty years have been called into question but no satisfactory new framework has been offered. Some years ago the principal foreign policy justification for foreign aid was to halt the spread of communism. There seemed then to be a strong, coordinated effort directed from Moscow to advance the cause of communism in the developing countries, and there was a general consensus that U.S. aid was needed to counteract the possibility of communist leaders seizing power in country after country by exploiting the poverty and misery of the bulk of their populations.

The threat of communism looks different today. The rapid changes in Eastern Europe have demonstrated the possibility of evolution within communist states toward greater freedom and diversity, even though the Soviet leaders are grimly trying to slow down the process. The split between the Soviet Union and China has shown that there is no simple, monolithic communist campaign. Events in a dozen countries have made it plain that nationalism is a more potent force than international communism, and only where local communist leaders have successfully identified themselves with nationalist aspirations have they made much headway.

None of this means that poverty and misery are no longer serious problems, or that communist leaders are not seeking to exploit them to seize power. But the threat to U.S. interests is plainly different if what we face is the possibility of numerous separate efforts at communist takeover in a wide variety of countries in various parts of the world, rather than a powerful, centrally-directed campaign to achieve the steady expansion of Soviet power. U.S. interests are clearly affected in both cases, but in different ways and with a different degree of urgency.

A second major challenge to the foundations of U.S. foreign policy since World War II has resulted from the Vietnamese war. Some have argued that the war raises serious questions about U.S. foreign assistance because it was through economic and military aid that we first became involved in Vietnam, and once entangled through our aid programs we could not later extricate ourselves. This argument is not persuasive even on superficial examination. There are dozens of countries in which the United States has conducted economic and/or military aid programs where conflict of one kind or another has broken out without entangling us—Pakistan, India, Jordan, the UAR, the Congo, Nigeria, and many more would illustrate the point. Nor is there evidence that we could not have extricated ourselves from Vietnam, had we wished to do so, at any point along the road to deeper involvement. The foreign aid program clearly did not "trap" us in Vietnam.

The real relationship between U.S. foreign aid and our involvement in Vietnam is a different one. Both are expressions of a foreign policy of active participation in world affairs—of a willingness vigorously and actively to use U.S. resources, including where judged necessary military force, to advance what are believed to be the interests of peace and progress. The United States did not become involved in the Vietnam war because we were trapped by foreign aid or by anything else; we became involved as a result of a series of deliberate decisions in which successive Presidents, on the advice of their senior colleagues in the Congress and in the Executive Branch, concluded that U.S. interests were at stake of sufficient importance to warrant the commitment of increasing amounts of resources including eventually combat forces.

It is this judgment which has been challenged with increasing vigor within the United States. Are the U.S. interests involved in Southeast Asia important enough to warrant the commitment of men and money we have made there? Even if important U.S. inter- ests are involved, do we have the influence, the power, and the know-how to intervene successfully and to bring about the outcome we desire?

It is important to note that these questions can be asked without necessarily challenging the premises of a foreign policy based on vigorous and active participation in the world. Mr. George Ball and Professor J. Kenneth Galbraith, for example, are two very different men who would probably agree that while the U.S. became over- committed in Vietnam, the remedy is not to give up all efforts by the United States to influence world events. Indeed, with respect to foreign aid, both would argue that the U.S. should do more and not less.

There are other critics of the Vietnamese war, however, such as Senator Fulbright, who see our involvement there as symptomatic of a U.S. readiness to participate too actively and too deeply in the affairs of other nations. Senator Fulbright and others who think as he does believe our foreign policy is not basically sound, but leads us to intervene far too much in matters we cannot materially influence, and to become involved in internal and external quarrels in other countries to the detriment of our true long-run interests. They specifically include our foreign aid program, as well as our Vietnamese policy and our various mutual defense alliances, in the ambit of this criticism.

To discuss this issue fully would require attention to elements of U.S. foreign aid, such as the provision of training and equip- ment for military forces, which are beyond the scope of a chapter concerned with population and food supplies. So far as economic assistance is concerned, however, the issue must be faced here. There is no doubt that the effective provision of foreign assistance for economic development necessarily involves not only the supply of resources but active participation by the suppliers of assistance in decisions on how the resources will be used. This is true whether the aid is provided through a national agency such as the U.S.

Agency for International Development or through an international agency such as the World Bank.

The reasons are plain. If an individual project is in question—a power plant, an irrigation system, an agricultural experiment station, an engineering college—the experience of all aid-giving agencies has clearly demonstrated that to achieve good results there must be a careful process of discussion and joint planning, testing and refining ideas involving not only how the external aid will be used but also how the local resources will be used.

The same point is true of large scale cases as well. When major assistance is under consideration for an economy (from an international bank, a national aid program, or a group of donors), experience has demonstrated the value of thorough discussions between recipient and donors about the development policies of the country in question. In the case of India, in 1964 and 1965, for example, there were numerous discussions among the Indian Government, the World Bank, and U.S. and other government aid agencies, centering on the priority that ought to be given to agriculture in India's development efforts, and by what means that priority should be given effect—questions which were crucial to the prospects for successful economic growth in India, and by the same token, to the prospects for successful use of the foreign assistance funds being discussed.

Does this process involve unwarranted intervention by outsiders in the internal affairs of aid-receiving countries—and intervention, indeed, in a rather ugly sense of pressure by the stronger on the weaker? Most of those who have been involved in recent years would deny the charge, for several reasons. Answers to the questions involved rest on technical analysis of the best means to achieve economic growth, and to an increasing extent major issues of development policy are being answered in approximately the same way by the economists and policymakers of both the advanced and the developing countries. Thus the dialogue between aid-giver and aid-receiver to a large extent—a conspicuously greater extent than was true, say, ten years ago—can be not a battle to see whose ideas will prevail but a constructive joint search for the best solution to a problem.

Even more important, the process rests on a basic mutuality of interest. Aid-giver and aid-receiver are both seeking rapid economic progress in the aid-receiving country. There is no doubt that the process of joint discussion outlined above involves the considera- tion by aid-giving organizations of issues of internal policy in aid- receiving countries, and some degree of influence by outsiders on the outcome. But the process, if handled sensibly, is more correctly described as an international process of cooperation toward mutu- ally-agreed ends than as a unilateral process of intervention. Each side retains the power of decision. Neither donor nor recipient is forced to reach agreement; either can decide to stop discussions and to terminate the flow of aid. Both are under pressure to reach agree- ment—the aid-receiver because he needs the assistance, the aid- giver because he has a strong interest in the solution of the problem to which the aid will be addressed. (These motivations are not as asymmetrical as they may seem at first glance, as witness the many occasions over the past decade on which hard bargainers from de- veloping countries have obtained aid without first having had to agree to any significant improvement in development policies.)

Taken all in all, therefore, it seems feasible to envision a process of giving and receiving aid which involves a great deal of joint discussion of development policy between aid-receivers and aid- donors but which need not involve improper infringement on the independence of aid-receiving countries. Such discussions are not of benefit only to donors. Often the issues involved are being more or less hotly debated inside an aid-receiving country, and insofar as the ideas of aid-givers are sound and constructive they will con- tribute to a favorable outcome of the internal debate. The views of aid-givers will not of course always be wise, and a considerable degree of humility about his understanding of another society is necessary in an effective aid-giver. For obvious reasons the aid dialogue is most comfortably conducted by officers of international agencies rather than by representatives of any one government, al- though this cannot always be arranged.

Recognizing all these qualifications, the fundamental fact re- mains that the provision of economic aid is not only tolerable but welcome to developing countries because it is aimed at helping them to achieve self-sustaining economic growth—which is to say, a position of economic independence in the world. They do not support the view that U.S. foreign aid should be reduced or eliminated on the grounds that it involves improper intervention. On the contrary, they strongly hope that assistance can be increased.

THE FUNDAMENTAL ISSUE

Why should the United States care? It is far beyond the scope of this chapter to propose a comprehensive and up-to-date framework for U.S. foreign policy. It is necessary for us, however, to suggest an answer to the question: how far do U.S. interests require us to provide the developing countries with assistance of the kind outlined above in solving their food and population problems? We offer the following outline of an answer:

1. We support an investment type of economic assistance, designed to produce self-sustaining results and requiring therefore high standards of self-help on the part of aid-receivers, provided to the maximum extent possible within a multilateral framework and under the leadership of international organizations. We support such assistance in a magnitude sufficient, if matched by appropriate assistance from other advanced countries and by appropriate self-help measures on the part of developing countries, to support steady and rapid progress toward self-sustaining growth. The probable magnitudes implied by this standard were indicated earlier in this chapter.

2. Such a foreign assistance effort, sustained over a period of years, offers the following potential benefits to the United States:

a. U.S. assistance can significantly reduce the chances of widespread suffering and famine within the next decade or two. If such suffering and famine occurred, they would surely require major relief expenditures from the United States. Moreover, they would undoubtedly result in great unrest and disruption in the affairs of many nations, which could only be damaging to the prospects for peaceful progress in the world that is so important to U.S. interests.

b. Moreover, U.S. assistance can ensure rapid economic progress in many developing countries which would otherwise grow slowly or not at all. This more rapid growth is clearly to the economic advantage of the United States because it opens larger opportunities for trade and for foreign investment, and because it increases the number of talented innovators seeking solutions to economic problems.

c. Furthermore—perhaps with less certainty—U.S. assistance by helping to achieve self-sustaining economic growth and by helping to solve urgent problems of food and population growth can contribute to a harmony of interest among many countries and the non-violent resolution of international disputes. We do not assert that economic progress automatically leads to political stability and peaceful intent—there is much evidence against such a thesis in the history of advanced as well as developing countries. We do suggest, however, that any country which is making good economic progress and is not facing crisis problems such as famine, or massive and increasing unemployment, has in fact a large stake in harmonious international relations and is more likely than otherwise to participate in constructive cooperative action with others. Insofar as this is true, it is a valuable step toward the kind of international environment most satisfactory for the United States.

d. Finally—and with even less certainty—it seems likely that U.S. assistance of the type and scale suggested would contribute significantly to the development of pluralistic economies and societies, conducive to the types of value systems and political institutions most congenial to our own. Again this is not an assertion of economic determinism, but only that U.S. aid has always had a natural bias towards reliance on the market rather than on governmental management, on private and cooperative as against state-owned enterprise, on widespread distribution of benefits rather than monopolistic gains—and in supporting policies and programs tending in these directions United States aid contributes to the spread of democratic and pluralistic values and institutions.

To the authors of this chapter these potential gains from strong and effective U.S. foreign assistance make in total an impressive case. There are a great many international issues which will not be solved by economic progress. But problems of hunger, and ignorance, and illness require economic advance for their solution. And the advantages to the United States of living in a world in which these problems are being met, as against living in a world in which they are festering unsolved, would seem to us to outweigh by far the projected costs.

Will these arguments prevail with the Congress and the public? We are not sure. The specter of hunger and over-population surely will not have the fearful impact on people's imagination that the specter of aggressive Soviet communism had in the 1950's. Nor, probably, will a measured case for carefully tailored assistance, dependent on negotiated relationships between self-help by recipients and cooperative action by donors, have the superficial appeal of past crusades against communism. This is, however, what seems to us to be called for by a realistic assessment of the requirements of the developing countries and the interests of the United States. And it has the advantage of offering a definite and clear-cut program of action leading to substantial progress.

Index

The American Assembly holds meetings of national leaders and publishes books to illuminate issues of United States policy. The Assembly is a national, non-partisan educational institution, incorporated in the State of New York.

The Trustees of the Assembly approve a topic for presentation in a background book, authoritatively designed and written to aid deliberations at national Assembly sessions at Arden House, the Harriman (N.Y.) Campus of Columbia University. These books are also used to support discussion at regional Assembly sessions and to evoke considerations by the general public.

All sessions of the Assembly, whether international, national, or local, issue and publicize independent reports of conclusions and recommendations on the topic at hand.

American Assembly books are purchased and put to use by thousands of individuals, libraries, businesses, public agencies, nongovernmental organizations, educational institutions, discussion meetings, and service groups.

The subjects of Assembly studies to date are:

1951————United States–Western Europe Relationships
1952————Inflation
1953————Economic Security for Americans
1954————The United States Stake in the United Nations
————The Federal Government Service
1955————United States Agriculture
————The Forty-Eight States
1956————The Representation of the United States Abroad
————The United States and the Far East
1957————International Stability and Progress
————Atoms for Power
1958————The United States and Africa
————United States Monetary Policy
1959————Wages, Prices, Profits, and Productivity
————The United States and Latin America
1960————The Federal Government and Higher Education
————The Secretary of State
————Goals for Americans
1961————Arms Control: Issues for the Public
————Outer Space: Prospects for Man and Society

1962———Automation and Technological Change
———Cultural Affairs and Foreign Relations
1963———The Population Dilemma
———The United States and the Middle East
1964———The United States and Canada
———The Congress and America's Future
1965———The Courts, the Public and the Law Explosion
———The United States and Japan
1966———The United States and the Philippines
———State Legislatures in American Politics
———A World of Nuclear Powers?
———Population Dilemma in Latin America
———Challenges to Collective Bargaining
1967———The United States and Eastern Europe
———Ombudsmen for American Government?
1968———Uses of the Seas
———Law in a Changing America
———Overcoming World Hunger
1969———Black Capitalism

Second Editions:

1962———The United States and the Far East
1963———The United States and Latin America
———The United States and Africa
1964———United States Monetary Policy
1965———The Federal Government Service
———The Representation of the United States Abroad
1968———Outer Space: Prospects for Man and Society
———Cultural Affairs and Foreign Relations
1969———The Population Dilemma